Front Cover: Adrian Gjertsen airborne in the Golden Apple Trust's F-86A Sabre from Bournemouth for an exclusive photographic sortie for Warbirds Worldwide. JOHN DIBBS PHOTOGRAPH EXCLUSIVELY FOR WARBIRDS WORLDWIDE.
This Page: Golden Hawks Sabres in an interesting formation exercise (Adrian Balch Collection)

WARBIRDS
W O R L D W I D E

WARBIRDS TODAY SERIES No.3
F-86 SABRE

EDITORIAL
Editorial Director/Publisher: Paul A. Coggan

Editorial Address: P.O. Box 99., Mansfield, Notts NG19 9GU, ENGLAND
Tel: (0623) 24288 Fax(0623) 22659

Financial Adviser: Philip S. Warner F.C.A.

Technical Illustrator: Terry Lawless

Chief Contributor

Duncan Curtis

Feature Writers

Adrian Gjertsen
James Kightly
Ed Horkey
Adrian Balch
Bob Becker
Skip Stagg
Ed Buerckholtz
Sqn Ldr P Frawley RAAF

Additional Material

John Dibbs
Gerry Manning

CONTENTS

INTRODUCTION

When I started to put this latest volume in the *Warbirds Today Series* together I thought I knew a little bit about the North American Aviation F-86 and its cousins. To be truthful, I now know a lot more.

Publication is quite a complex process. Take close to 50,000 words, a handful of enthusiastic Sabre specialists, a guy floating around in a Jet Provost manoeuvring to get pictures of a graceful and rare F-86A, and a not inconsiderable amount of technology and mix together. Garnish with many hours of labour, an attempt to bolster yet further the profits of *British Telecom* and a few mild panics. Travel several miles by German built motor vehicle to see gentlemen with a Japanese scanner and German printing machines and you have it. All achieved with the help of an American conceived computer assembled in Ireland. Truly an international effort. One thing I forgot to

mention - the two humans at *Warbirds Worldwide*.

* * * * * * * * * * * * * * * * * * * *

The North American Sabre is far from extinct. Indeed the type is still being operated today in military service in Bolivia, performing a variety of tasks associated with the military. What is even more exciting is the amount of activity surrounding the rebuilding of the type as a warbird, and again this effort is truly worldwide. There are literally tons of spares, and a significant number of airframes in a varying conditions and a growing number of companies offering Sabre Jet related services.

When I visited Italy several years ago I witnessed a sight that filled me full of sadness, and yet it is a sight many others have seen and have got off their backsides and done something about. In the scrapyard at Castrette there lay a number of battered, truly de-milled and rotting F-86Ks. The wings had been punctured

at carefully measured intervals with a terrifying precision. Spars had been cut, and other important components mutilated. The problem is there is no shortage of Sabre jets, and so no need, one may think, to preserve any aircraft about to be retired from the military. The warbird jet movement is still in its infancy, but it is, due to the labours of a few individuals overcoming attempts at unfair restrictions and has openly rebelled against attempts by bureaucrats to restrict operations, largely by self regulation and active lobbying of officials at all levels.

The myths surrounding the accident at Sacramento does nothing to enhance the image of the Sabre jet. Very recently, I read with horror a brief but inaccurate report on this incident. In 1989 I had the pleasure of meeting a man who was, and still is, a part of *North American Aviation's* history - Ed Horkey. When you get to know Ed, it is not difficult to under-

a Charter Member. CJFM is now at EAA Oshkosh, and the CJAA have recently been adopted by the *Experimental Aircraft Association*. Together, the EAA and CJAA will ensure the safety of the future of the jet warbird movement in the U.S.A. and this will have favourable repercussions worldwide.

I'd like to thank all those people - our contributors - who submitted material and gave me the final push to produce the latest in the series. This publication also marks a first for us, and our newly appointed Technical Illustrator, Terry Lawless. Terry spent over 300 hours on the airbrushed cutaway of *Golden Apple's* unique North American Aviation F-86A Sabre, G-SABR, shown on page 16 and 17, and we decided to produce a super-limited edition print of this magnificent work. It will in fact be very limited - 86 prints! Details on page 21.

Many years ago, we thought we might be taking a risk when we published JETS - only our second special edition. Suffice to say it carried a CAC Sabre on the cover, and it sold very quickly. Now, unlike the Sabre, it's extinct!

SABRE JET CLASSICS

For those of you that lust for more information on the F-86 and its variants a publication called Sabre Jet Classics is essential. Produced by Rick Mitchell of SABRE JET HISTORICAL SOCIETY, 428 Madingley Road, Linthicum, MD 21090, U.S.A. annual dues are just $16.00. This is an excellent publication in every respect and is filled with interesting, previously unpublished information.

*Left: This Canadair CL-13B is shown at Chino in 1977. This aircraft became N86CD with Corwin Denney in 1986 then N30CJ with Corporate Jet, flying targets at Decci, Sardinia then Soesterburg, Holland until it and N50CJ returned to the U.S.A. **Below:** This CL-13 was not so lucky, ending up, as the picture shows, being scrapped(MAP via Duncan Curtis)*

stand how, with this calibre of person directly employed in important decision making, N.A.A. succeeded in producing so many fine fighters. The Sabre was amongst them. Ed promised to send me data on the famous Ice Cream Parlour incident. The sad fact is, over the years myths have been perpetuated about the Sacramento incident. I hope, once and for all, with Ed's help (due to his personal involvement with the court proceedings following the incident), we can set the record straight.

Some time after the Italian trip I visited Houston, Texas, then the home of the *Combat Jets Flying Museum* and was inspired by the ideas and energy of Jim Robinson. The CJFM had two Canadair Sabres, and a very positive attitude toward Jet operations. Also closely involved with this jet operation was Chuck Parnall, who, though he will deny it, was the hard, driving force behind the U.S. based *Classic Jet Aircraft Association*, of which I am proud to be

Adrian Gjertsen takes us on a flight in the UK's only resident F86 - the rare A model G-SABR Exclusive Photography by **John Dibbs**

"I cannot remember exactly how Kasler looked. The image is like a dream just at the moment it begins to be lost in the light of day. He had a round head, thin lips, and cold uninquisitive gaze. He was laconic, the words barely slipping from his mouth, and he had dignity, from what who knows. Skill of course, great natural as well as acquired skill, together with nerve, and a burning patience. Crowning it all was the unsentimentality of a champion, an air of indestructibility standing against aimlessness and indifference".

A vivid and memorable description by a young, newly-arrived pilot on meeting his first 'combat ace' when joining his Sabre squadron on the 4th Fighter Interceptor Wing, Korea in 1950.

The Korean War produced many aces. After less than a month flying on his hero's wing, this young pilot was himself an ace, cast in the same mould - his trusty steed - the vastly out-numbered North American F-86A Sabre, his combatant - the MiG-15, and the theatre - over the river Yalu, North Korea, in the infamous MiG Alley.

This was still the era of fighter aces, the fig-ures speak for themselves - 87,000 missions, 792 MiG15 kills for 78 Sabres - a kill ratio of over 10 to 1. It must have been an extraordi-nary time to have been flying, with little room for those of a nervous disposition, and many of the stories have passed into legend.

To early Hollywood movie buffs the film *The Ice-Man Cometh*, an F-86 squadron com-mander's battle to pull his Sabre squadron out of their state of low morale and combat nerves, was the essence of that young ace's reminis-cences, with stunning air-to-air footage of Sabres punching off drop-tanks as they engaged enemy MiG-15's. It made a lasting impression on me any way, and since then I have always wanted to fly the Sabre.

In April 1992, some 42 years plus from the date of its first operational sortie in Korea, I had the chance to fulfil that wish at Bournemouth, and not just in any old Sabre, but an F-86A model - vanquisher of MiG Alley and currently the only airworthy A model F-86 left in the world. It was also the model that achieved a world speed record of 671 mph in 1948 - the year I was born.

Some aircraft look ugly, most look functional, and a handful look 'real good'. The Sabre falls

Flying the MiG KILLI

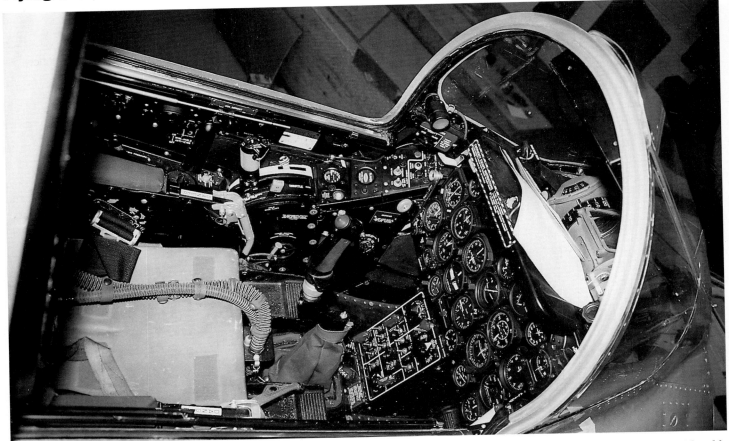

Top: *The F-86A's cockpit. Considerable work was undertaken by Fort Wayne Air Service at Baer Field, Fort Wayne, Indiana on the A model Sabre before it was imported to the U.K. This included returning much of the cockpit back to its original stock military condition. (Duncan Curtis).*

into this last category. The first impression is that it appears somewhat short-coupled, aggressively functional and quite the metal of which legends are born.

Apart from how to operate it, an aircraft's pilots manual quite often gives some insight into the machine itself, or at least its pedigree. The Sabre's manual is an eye opener and the first thing that is apparent is that this is a *real* first generation jet . The pages are liberally sprinkled with *Warning* and *Caution* boxes with curt explanations beneath. Many of these would be taken for granted today.

The engine - a General Electric J-47 - was the first operational axial flow jet into service and the manual goes to some lengths to explain its operation and limitations. The ejection seat is also first-of-a-kind, the instrumentation very comprehensive for an early jet but hardly ergonomic like today's, and the Sabre's handling and performance are covered in a way only the Americans can do.

So what is it like to fly for the first time? On approaching the aircraft to complete the external inspection, the most noticeable thing is the cavernous intake in its nose. On peering down the intake, the trunking runs back into the bowels of the fuselage, passing under the floor of the cockpit, up a slope and into the jaws of the J-47 compressor, situated at about mid-span of the wings. So the whole front half of the Sabre is nothing more than a huge hollow tube around the intake duct.

The wing leading edge slats on most Sabres are invariably beautifully polished, and on this particular aircraft the movable slats have been immobilised and are permanently retracted.

The rest of the external is unremarkable, with few differences from any other early jet. It is only when seated in the cockpit that some of the other noteworthy features for an aircraft of its era become apparent. The single most striking feature sitting perched on the ejection seat is one that has become the hallmark of US fighters to this day - exceptional visibility. The canopy protrudes well clear of the fuselage, the sitting position is high, and all-round visibility is magnificent. The ejection seat is very unlike Mr. Martin Baker's and shows its early design characteristics. There are two stirrups into which to place your heels in the event of ejection, and two firing handles, one either side of the seat, which are operated as levers with guarded triggers.The parachute is separate, has explosive deployment charges inside it, and is buckled on before entering the aircraft. The seat parameters are a minimum height of 500 feet straight and level, and speed in excess of 90 knots.

The instrument panel is a packed cluster of dials, and most are fairly standard presentations, apart from the compass, which takes a little getting used to. It is basically a fixed compass card with cardinal headings as one would expect, North at the top, South at the bottom etc, but the aircraft magnetic heading is indicated by a pointer that rotates to the relevant heading. Easy to interpret when flying due North or South, but requiring a little more thought when flying East or West to avoid disorientation.

So on to engine start-up. This is perhaps the single trickiest part of operating the Sabre, and needs to be performed with great care plus

something of a instinctual feel. The J-47 is a very early jet engine, and has few of the sophisticated engine fuel and barometric flow-control units that have become the norm today, where throttle inputs are tailored automatically to suit aircraft and engine conditions. With the J-47, the pilot's left hand takes the place of the sophisticated flow control units. Throttle movement directly controls fuel input, and a heavy hand below 70% rpm is likely to overtemp the turbine and leave a molten mess at the bottom of the jet-pipe. Starting requires two hands on the throttle, and very gentle movements feeding fuel into the combustion chambers, just sufficient to sustain combustion and allow painfully slow acceleration up to idling rpm, but not so much as to overtemp the turbine. Once idling, the oil pressure is an alarmingly meagre 2psi., hardly registering on the gauge.

With the engine running and internal checks performed, including a thorough check of the hydraulically boosted flying controls, taxying is straightforward using the hydraulic nose-wheel steering. Pre-takeoff checks complete at the holding point, it only remains to carry-out a check of the emergency fuel control system at full power, once lined up on the runway. This is an important check and takes about a minute and a half to complete, during which time the ky behind the aircraft fills with billowing black exhaust fumes that are a characteristic of the Sabre.

Brakes released and the Sabre is relatively low to accelerate by modern jet standards with only 5,200 pounds of thrust. The stop-go bort point passes but acceleration is still noticeably sluggish. Nosewheel liftoff is at 105 knots followed shortly thereafter by the main-wheels at 125 knots. The book gives a ground run of 3,000 feet with full fuel on a standard 15°C, still air day, though it feels it is going to use a lot more. Advice from one or two of the Korean aces makes a minimum of 6,000 feet of runway appear to be a good baseline, but rather longer than might be expected. Most early jets tend to use more runway to stop on landing than for take-off, but the Sabre is an exception using more for take-off, than that required for landing.

Once in the air the undercarriage is raised before airspeed reaches 185 knots. This is accomplished by using the American style gear-lever which is then placed back to the centre 'combat' or 'hold' position to release pressure from the system. A similar process applies to the flaps, and airbrakes, with all selections followed by the 'combat' or 'hold' position to release system pressure.

Acceleration to a climbing speed of 350 knots and a 80-90 degree angle-of-bank turn to leave the circuit immediately brings in the noticeable 'thruppenny bit' movement of the ailerons due to the boosted controls. This system is somewhat different to the usual hydraulically assisted flying controls. Hydraulic power is only supplied to the controls when there is a greater force exerted externally on the control surfaces, so produces a somewhat uneven application of hydraulic boost giving it the distinctive 'thruppenny bit' feel, or slightly lumpy rocking motion both in pitch and roll, particularly at lower speeds.

A clearing glance over the shoulder provides a magnificent view all the way round to past the 6 o'clock position. Visibility is superb and the USAF markings on the wing an unusual thrill. Climb to medium level and a clear area 35 miles to the West of the airfield is accomplished in less than 5 minutes.

Clearing turns, followed by security and airframe checks, with the throttle at idle and speed decaying towards 150 knots, provides a chance to look at the clean stall characteristics. The blaring warning horn, for idle power without undercarriage, is startling, but once cancelled returns the cockpit to an eerie silence. The aircraft is heavy, with fuel still in the two 100 gallon drop tanks, when a mild buffet sets in at 134 knots, some 11 knots higher than if the slats were extended, followed by a nose drop at 124 knots. Release of the back pressure on the stick, and gentle application of power almost immediately removes the buffet, and stall recovery is accomplished with minimal loss of height. In a dirty configuration, with flap, undercarriage and airbrake, the speeds are some 10 knots lower and the buffet a little more masked - a real pussy-cat for such a high performer.

Cleaning up and accelerating to 300 knots for an examination of stall in manoeuvre, buffet and 4g are coincident as the speed decays whilst tightening the turn. It is not possible to examine the much publicised warning of 'tuck' at higher G's due to the 4g limit with drop tanks fitted. At war, full 7g manoeuvrability for combat was achieved by 'punching off' the drop tanks on engaging the enemy in a dog-fight. Another little Sabre quirk is the noticeable pitch-up when the airbrake is extended, which can add as much as 2-3 g to a manoeuvre, prompting the warning in the pilot's notes to 'be sure to extend the speed brakes before pulling out of a dive to avoid overstressing the airframe'!

Aerobatics are a joy, showing the full manoeuvrability of the Sabre. Slow rolls at 250 knots, barrel rolls at 300 knots, and loops at 350 knots, but care needs to be taken not to exceed that somewhat limiting 4g with tanks on, and a similarly limiting 3 seconds inverted flight capability.

Throughout these manoeuvres, the aircon-ditioning and pressurisation surges with power application, playing havoc with sensitive ears. Temperature control is good but the cabin altimeter whirls up and down several thousand feet at a time with each power change. It is a primitive but functional system, with little between the engine compressor tapping and the cockpit outlet. Engine response above 70 percent is excellent, but below that is extremely poor, with great care required until the magic 70 percent is reached.

Return to an empty circuit at 350 knots cruise takes less than 5 minutes again, with little time to admire the magnificent view of Poole

Top: The classic lines of this real first generation jet are shown to advantage in this unique shot taken from a Jet provost camera ship. Originally the aircraft was painted with black and yellow stripes but the error was corrected by Jet Heritage following research by the owner.

Flying the MiG Killer

Top: *Visibility from the F-86 is magnificent, as can be seen from this shot looking up at the pilot. Also emphasised is the size of the cavernous air intake, the hallmark of the main models of the F-86.*

Harbour to the North, and Studland Bay beneath.

Pattern speed is 170 knots downwind, reducing to 150 knots on the base turn and finals. The final approach is flown with gear, flap and airbrake to keep the J-47 spooled up for fast response in the event of a go-around, and speed across the fence is 125 knots at this weight. A go-around requires some coordination - power up - airbrake in - gear up - flap up - throttle back - gear to combat - flap to combat - and turn downwind at 170 knots. Downwind landing checks, finals turn, across the fence at 125 knots again, and the aircraft settles firmly onto the runway at 115 knots. It is easy to control with its wide track undercarriage, and the brakes are excellent.

Turning off the runway, after landing checks complete, and taxying back to the dispersal, it is impossible to avoid an ear-to-ear grin. The manual requires a minimum of one minute run up to 70 percent rpm for oil scavenging before

shut-down, so a clear area behind is essential. Shutdown itself requires a little consideration, and care has to be taken to prevent fuel pump-

ing into the hot jet-pipe during run down causing a turbine fire, a common Sabre problem.

With the seat made safe, internal shutdow complete, mic-tel, g-suit and straps discon nected, the grin is still firmly in place. Standin up in the cockpit somewhat awkwardly, wit parachute still buckled, to survey the aircra provides a real sense of well-being. It is a exhilarating aircraft to fly, a real performer bu docile enough to handle. There are still a cor siderable number of current military jets, som four decades down the line, that have nothin like the Sabre's performance

Finally, with feet firmly on the ground agair parachute over the shoulder, and some 40 gallons of fuel used for 45 minutes airborn time, it has been a fulfiled ambition. It is goin to be a real pleasure working up a low-level dis play routine.

Left: *Adrian Gjertsen at the controls of G SABR during the photographic sort mounted for The Golden Apple Trust an Warbirds Worldwide.*

The Sabre has its quirks, and displays idiosyncrasies due to its age and early stage of jet aircraft development, but it is a fine machine all round. That it was so successful in Korea speaks volumes for its pedigree, but having flown it now, I can say without fear of contradiction, that it says volumes more for the men who flew it in anger over the river Yalu in 'MiG Alley' forty years ago. And what of the vanquished foe and their steed, the worthy MiG-15? Anyone got one of those I can fly to compare with the Sabre?! Adrian Gjertsen Operations Director and Chief Pilot Jet Heritage.

G-SABR is operated by Jet Heritage on behalf of The Golden Apple Trust. Air Show bookings can be made by contacting Vic Norman at Rendcomb on 0285 831774 or by Fax on 0285 831747

bove: This unusual almost documentary type shot illustrates the Sabres classic lines and, a certain extent the jet fighters Mustang ancestry. The aircraft is currently painted in a Korean theatre scheme but service with both the Californian and Washington Air National Guard units may prompt the owners to change at a later date to reflect this service.

Shattered Dreams

James Kightly looks back at the plans of the Haydon Baillie Aircraft & Naval Collection to fly a Canadair Sabre in the UK in the early 1970's

On July 3rd 1977, P-51D Mustang I-BILL crashed at Mainz, West Germany, whilst in the circuit. The pilot and passenger were both killed. This tragedy was to put a premature end to not only two young lives, but one of the most ambitious aircraft collections in the world.

The pilot of the Mustang was Ormond Haydon Baillie, a man who many will need no introduction to, but in the briefest of character sketches had been one of the great display pilots of his generation. Though an Englishman, he had flown in the Royal Canadian Air Force, and discovering an interest in warbirds he proceeded to build up a remarkable collection of them. First was an ex Royal Australian Navy Hawker Sea Fury, WH589 which Ormond took to the United States and proceeded to race with success in the wide variety of events open at that time.

It was, however, to Britain that he eventually brought the aircraft, and once here he began building what was then a unique collection of types, choosing the then dormant Duxford Airfield as his operating base. Naming it the *Haydon-Baillie Aircraft & Naval Collection*, in association with his brother Wensley, the next step was to purchase two Canadair Silver Stars which became the *Black Knights Aerobatic Team*, and by mid 1977 the collection consisted of over twenty five airframes.

As an ex RCAF pilot Ormond had a great affec

piston success with the jet environment which was open then. A number of engines and spares were also acquired from Erding and Gilching AF bases and the collection was looking extremely healthy with the 'missing' Spitfire that the collection desperately wanted being 'found' in India (along with seven others).

Then in July 1977 came the blow. Ormond was killed and the collection lost its chief pilot, engineer and driving force in one blow. Wensley Haydon-Baillie was left with a batch of various marks of derelict Spitfire scattered all over India, which had just been acquired, the Sea Fury, currently in Germany, as well as Five Sabres with spares for all these types also scattered world wide and time to bring them back to the UK extremely limited.

Naturally, the recovery of the Spitfires took priority, and from October 1977 until the new year, the hand-picked team were in India, learning about how (and how not to) recover aircraft. After the Spitfires were safely back in Britain thoughts turned urgently towards the Sabres. Time was in fact running out, as a deadline had been set for the removal of the aircraft, and partly because of this, and also because of the deterioration suffered by the Messerschmitt aircraft it was decided to dismantle them all and bring them to Wroughton (chosen as space at Duxford was running out) in crates. A mobile home was chosen as a major cost saver for the team, who arrived in Germany in March, and by October, 1978, all five Sabre airframes were back in the UK. Much time had been saved by the experience gained in the Indian expedition and the help given by the Luftwaffe, M.B.B. and Dornier. As ever, in any forward thinking organisation, in addition to the airframes there was a large spares holding including a number of Orenda engines which the five engineless ex Dornier aircraft would need. At this stage the intention was still to fly one Sabre, restoring one to static and use the rest as spares, but sadly this was never to be. In April 1979 all the aircraft had been shipped to *Flight Systems Inc.* at Mojave, California, to join the huge number of Sabres

being operated by that company.

By the end of 1992, three of the five aircraft were still extant, two having been written off. This was only part of the *Haydon-Baillie Aircraft and Naval Collection* dream, and in the jet arena alone they had managed to get a CF-100 Cannuck operating (the only example airworthy in Europe, and the only civil Cannuck ever), acquired three Canadair Silver Stars in what was clearly only the beginning of an innovative jet display team (interestingly one of these aircraft is now back at Duxford in the hands of the *Old Flying Machine Company*) and two Meteor jet fighters with the aim of putting them back in the air too. This was in the era when few in Britain conceived of operating a single civil jet warbird seriously, never mind a collection.

A lot more died in the crash of Mustang I-BILL than a great pilot and his passenger; the kingpin of a warbird collection which was clearly only in its formative stages, yet was already a unique world leader. What might have happened can only be speculated about, but it would definitely have been a sight to see Ormond Haydon-Baillie in an all black Canadair Sabre low and fast at Duxford....................**WW James Kightly.**

Left: The Canadair CL-13B Mk 6 c/n 1675 was built for the Luftwaffe, and first flew on 11th February 1958. It was delivered to the Luftwaffe as JD-103 and was operated by 1st Staffel of JG74. It became BB-284 of Waffenschule 10 and then passed to Messerschmitt as KE104 and used as a chase plane during VJ-101 VTOL Fighter programme around 1964. In the late 1960's the aircraft passed on to the Test Centre at Erprobungstelle 61, Manching as 0113. It was sold to Ormond Haydon Baillie and later stored at Wroughton. Following shipment to the USA it was registered N1039K, and later N80FS. The Martin Baker Mk 5 seat replaced the C-2 on many Luftwaffe Sabres from 1960. Martin baker equipped Sabres have a revised canopy opening mechanism to clear the seat, plus additional rear view Mirrors (MAP via Duncan Curtis) Below: A Luftwaffe Canadair CL-13B Sabre 6 at Fassberg on 4th June 1983 - though not a Haydon Baillie aircraft (Gerry Manning)

on for the Canadair Sabre, ideal for a flamboyant man like Ormond to fly in shows and ces. There would be no doubt that if the opportunity arose he would buy one. The opportunity to purchase an example owned by *Messerschmitt-Bolkow-Blohm GmbH* in ermany came Ormond's way and he bought Four other airframes became available at ornier's base at Oberpfaffenhofen, and ough these were incomplete, lacking engines armament they were bought for the collection as spares backup for the original MBB rframe (c/n 1675) which was by this time ndergoing preliminary work to restore it to flyg condition with the aim of ferrying it to the .K.

The intention at this stage was to restore the rst aircraft and use it as an airshow mount in e U.K. probably also taking it to America for season of racing, hoping to repeat Ormond's

F-86A Sabre

U.S. AIRFORCE F-86A-7-NA
A.F. SERIAL № 48-178

North American Aviation
F-86A 48-178 G-SABR

The Myth

"The Canadian built Sabre had undesirable performance, stability and control characteristics that caused it to crash into an ice cream parlour in Sacramento, California, killing 22 people and injuring 25 more on September 24th 1972".

The Facts

The above statement is certainly one of the most inaccurate ever made about the Canadair Sabre, and, even twenty years on is still construed by many as accurate. Not only this, but it continues to be quoted, and highlighted in articles about the type and the modern jet warbird movement in general. Ed Horkey, a much respected aerodynamicist and a person very closely involved with the type during its development at North American Aviation takes up the story, based on his extensive and personal involvement with the case.

Shortly after the F-86 got under production in California, the Canadian government joined in and the F-86s were built under license at the Canadair facility. They started out first with the basic 'E' configuration and GE engines. However, later in the programme the Mark V configuration was more like the F-86H and also featured an Orenda engine. The episode being discussed here happened on a Canadair surplus airplane that had been purchased by a company and was being flown at an air show in Sacramento in 1972. An abstract of the accident report is shown on page 19. With so many people killed and injured, the lawyers involved had small teams set up for plaintiffs and defendants. The trial started and after a period of time it had more or less been settled, with a settlement approaching four million dollars. Sometime during the trial a so-called aerodynamicist from San Diego was called in. This guy, in my considered opinion, was actually a pathetic aerodynamicist; I have documentation to substantiate my claim. Furthermore,

with a Ph.D. degree from Italy, he had worked on transport wings at Convair. Since he was a foreigner he had *no security clearance and could not work on military aeroplanes*. His criticisms of the F-86 were based on hangar talk. In Arizona, in both the State and Federal Courts this man would not have been allowed to be classified as an expert. I have been an expert witness in about 150 trials and 250 depositions so I know. Likewise a pilot was selected who was a very good 'stick and rudder' man, but, again he was shy of any formal education or knowledge.

Part way through the trail a settlement had been decided upon among the lawyers of almost four million dollars, going against the two insurance companies of the pilot and the company that owned the aeroplane, the City and County of Sacramento and some others. Somewhere in this time span the inputs of the two unqualified 'experts' surfaced and gave the plaintiffs attorney's the idea that they could collect a lot more, maybe even double that amount. At this point, the lawyers representing the County and City of Sacramento contacted me. Word had finally gotten to them that I was a Chief Technical Engineer in charge of some 900 people when the F-86 was developed and might have some real *valid* inputs on it. I agreed to help and they sent me a large amount of data including the FAA reports, the manuals on the Orenda Sabre -5, depositions of the aerodynamics experts etc. I went through this data. First I got the airplane weights and temperatures and I figured out that the computed take-off roll was 3456 feet, and then if he had to chop the engine at that point the landing roll would have been another 3520 feet so I ended up with some 6976 feet which should have been his minimum runway requirement. *The runway he elected to use was only 5000 feet long*. He did not use the 10,000 feet runway because he might have had to wait 15 minutes for clearance and was afraid of running out of fuel to go to Oakland, his home base. With Oakland only 100 miles away, he was again wrong and would have had enough fuel for a 45 to 60 minute wait. The pilot, Bingham, had so little experience I'm sure he

didn't know how to use the manual. The people who checked him out probably didn't understand it either. It was a tragedy of errors in which incompetence played the major part. I then read aerodynamicist Dr. Garbell's comments and realised he was a pathetic expert.

I then approached North American Aviation which was the original designer of the F-86. Some of the old aerodynamicists who worked for me hauled out all their reports and showed me that the aeroplane had satisfactory performance. In fact, it was exceptionally good with the Orenda engine. It also met the stability and control criteria. As a government aeroplane this had to meet a Federal specification, R1815. For your education, what it says fundamentally is that you have to have adequate stability and control. Stability means that, for instance, if you are in a take off attitude and you pull back on the stick it takes a pull force; if you push forward on the stick, it takes a push force. All this crap that Garbel got into about over-rotation is just that, so much crap. I doubt if he knew about R1815. This also was something that the pilot expert they had, who said you had to be very well trained and had to be careful because the plane had a tendency to over rotate. Well Baloney, you couldn't have had that and meet the R1815 specification!

I then went to Irvine, California, and met with some people at *Flight Research Inc.* They were taking excess Canadair Sabres and converting them into drones for use by the Navy. You were to take the pilot out and fly the Sabre remotely and fire missiles at it. It had a miss distance indicator on it so you could save the airplane but you could tell how close the missile came to it. That way, you wouldn't have to keep shooting down expensive drones. They also commented that after they normally restored the Sabre to good condition and had a pilot fly it, they went ahead and put in the remote controls. All the pilots and people at *Flight Research* indicated that it was a hell of a good airplane, good performance, high stability and control.

I then visited China Lake where these drones were being used. It was very interesting. Here is a facility with a long runway and a blockhouse about a quarter of a mile from the end of the runway. A crewman would get into the Sabre and taxi it out to the end of the runway and then get out. From then on the controllers in the blockhouse with television cameras and feedback from the remote control systems would take the drone off, fly it, have a missile fired at it and then return and land it. What this short segment of movie they gave me showed that there was an airplane that if you could d

FACTS
FARRELL'S
ICE CREAM PARLOUR

hat, must be extremely reliable with no stability and control problems. I then proceeded to Sacramento where I met with some of the Defense attorneys; about a half dozen of them. I went through the technical data first to show them that they had been suckered by these phoney experts. I then showed them the China Lake movies. That was really the clincher. They said "God Ed, this is great. Be at the Courthouse in the morning and you'll be the first one to testify".

I arrived at the Courthouse in the morning, and all the lawyers, both plaintiff and Defense, went into the Judge's chambers. About an hour later, they came out. The Defense lawyers were all smiles and they came up to me and said "Ed, you've done it for us, in particular the China Lake movies, and we've convinced the plaintiff's attorneys that if you testify, with your legitimate data and drone movie, they'll be shot down, so they've agreed to go back to the original settlement and accept just under four million dollars. You're free to go home and send us your bill, and thanks a million".

Here again, this is a story you don't get from the media. What you get is the stuff that the airplane is suspected of being marginal, and so on, and what you don't get it the complicity of the FAA. Here they are licensing someone that should never have been licensed. They also get into the fact that the big deal about the difference in horizon between Oakland and Sacramento which is of interest only for an untrained pilot. They also bring out, but aren't very critical of themselves, in terms of letting the ice cream parlour be placed at the end of the runway. They are involved in licensing land around an airport! There has been a continuing battle between warbird owners and the FAA as to how these aircraft should be operated. In fact, the data I've presented here was used in a briefing at Pensacola almost two years ago where the FAA from Washington was in attendance. We tried to keep them from passing a regulation that warbird airplanes should have tanks bolted on. Now to me this is absolutely ridiculous. The chances of a pilot dropping an empty tank on a city is just one in ten million, whereas the extra drag and weight of a bolted on tank can easily be the difference between a survivable crash and one that is not. Likewise, they have also passed a law that you cannot use ejection seats. To me, this was absolutely insane. Way back in P-51 days, we were sorry we didn't have ejection seats. At the speeds involved, ejection seats were a Godsend.

The British Civil Aviation Authority is also picking on the warbirds and, in addition to bolting on tanks, they have also come up with the fact that you cannot fly a warbird that has independent hydraulic boosted control systems. It just so happens that practically all your transports that fly in the world today use this basic reliability criteria. Now here they are saying that if that type of system is on a warbird you cannot fly it, but it's OK to be on a Boeing 737 or an Airbus 300. No wonder this country and others are on the verge of going down the

tubes with some of the idiots that occupy bureaucratic positions.

Even more serious in the United States is the power of attorneys in recent years. They have hamstrung General Aviation with their product liability operations. Please note in this case that with almost 4 million going to the plaintiffs, their attorneys usually make 33 to 50% of the money. 4 divided by 3 equals 1,333,333.00 to be split. A warbird owner should therefore worry about his insurance and exposure to litigation. The FAA or CAA will not be of any help if one gets into trouble. **Ed Horkey**

$4 million
Settlement reached in air crash disaster

SACRAMENTO-An out of courts settlement of nearly $4 million has been reached in suits resulting from a Sacramento air crash disaster which killed 22 persons.

The money will be divided among the families of those killed and 25 injured in California's worst air-ground accident.

The accident occurred in September 1972, when a Canadian Mark V Sabre jet (F86) crashed into Farrell's Ice Cream Parlour in a shopping center adjacent to the Sacramento Executive airport.

The trial began last October to assess liability. A second phase would have been held to determine damages if the defendants and plaintiffs had not settled.

An attorney, Richard L. Bingham, pilot of the airplane, said the trial would probably have gone to mid-June on the liability issue with another three or four months of trial in the phase to determine damages.

Insurance companies for Bingham, 41, who survived, and Spectrum Air, owner of the jet, will pay $3,192,000 according to attorneys.

Others involved in the settlement and amounts they will pay are: the City and County of Sacramento, operators of the airport, $200,000; Farrell's: $100,000; the owners and developers of the shopping center, $200,000; State of California, $10,000 and sponsors of the air show at which Bingham performed $100,000.

The trial had been the longest in Sacramento history. The total award was also the highest in Sacramento history.

From Sacramento Newspaper July 76

Continued on Page 22

Report No: NTSB-AAR-73-6

Aircraft Accident Report:
Spectrum Air Inc.,Sabre Mk 5, N275X, Sacramento Executive Airport, Sacramento, California, Date: September 24th 1972

Report Date: March 28, 1973

Performing Organisation: National Transportation Safety Board.

Abstract (from Section 16): Spectrum Air Inc., Sabre Mk 5, N275X, crashed during a rejected takeoff from runway 30 at Sacramento Exec. Airport at approximately 1624 Pacific daylight time, on September 24th 1972. The aircraft collided with several automobiles and came to rest in an ice cream parlour across the street from the airport. Twenty-two persons on the ground were killed and 28 others, including the pilot, were injured. The aircraft was destroyed.

The aircraft became airborne twice during the attempted take-off, but each time returned to the runway. The pilot reported that the aircraft acceleration and control response were normal until he felt a vibration shortly after initial liftoff. He did not recall if it persisted through the subsequent liftoff and rejected takeoff.

The National Transportation Safety Board determines that the probable cause of this accident was the overrotation of the aircraft and subsequent derogation of the performance capability. The overrotation was the result of inadequate pilot proficiency in the aircraft and misleading visual clues.

Five recommendations were made to the FAA

Key Words: Overrotation, Inadequate proficiency, Surplus military aircraft

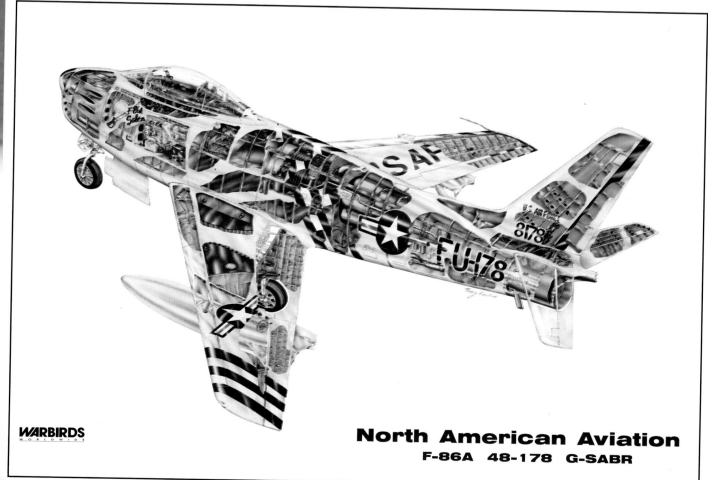

Left: Canadair Sabre Mk 5 ex RCAF 23315 being used as a QF-86E target drone. N275X was configured almost identically. (MAP Photo).

The Errors

Ed Horkey made several observations during and after the Sacramento trial and many are still valid today as potential pitfalls for the jet pilot

Bingham Training
The admission of only 3.5 hours (verifiable) and possibly four hours more of flights in the F-86 is frightening. However, even worse and more basic are the following:
a. None of the other personnel involved, such as the FAA representative involved, appear to have much of a background on the F-86. How could they train Mr. Bingham?
b. No training films were utilised although very good films are available.
c. None of the personnel involved seem to have much background in use of the flight operating instruction handbook. A pilot about to fly the F-86 should have understood the charts to the point where he could:
1 Evaluate fuel required for a flight from Sacramento to Oakland. Bingham claimed he had a 15 minute delay at the airport allowable. He had at least one hour.
2 Check out balanced runway concept and V nose lift off, V1 (speed of last decision), V lift off, V ground flaps up, V climb etc.
3 Bingham claims to have forgotten what he did but a trained person could use the charts and explain his analysis several years later. It is strongly suspected that he never understood the charts etc.
e. An experienced instructor should have been used.

Start of Take-off

A. He did not understand the trim functions. In his disposition he talked about trim light for neutral position. Actually, the horizontal trim should be full aft (stabiliser nose down). This gives correct feel for take-off roll and/or landing approaches. The proper trim can be ascertained by matching the stabiliser and geared elevator motion. Normal pull forces for take off then result.

B. He should have been told to assume a slightly nose-up attitude until the final take-off pull up.

Take Off

It is suspected that he knew he was marginal in terms of weight and take off performance and that this influenced him for an early take off more than the horizon angular differences between Oakland and Sacramento. Just prior to the accident, the closeness of a dike could well have become the main influence.

Aborting the take-off.

His dependence on aerodynamic drag versus braking forces was completely wrong. The balanced runway analysis should have been made prior to take off and would have told him this. Also a good instructor would know that he could not drop tanks (first emergency move normally made) as they were bolted on and would have recommended using wheel brakes and then raising the gear as the right emergency procedures.

Miscellaneous

The analysis of actual speeds and angles from the NTSB report appears to correspond to Bingham's inputs.

Comments on Dr. Garbell's Disposition

Wing shape in regards to stall was best on early F-86's, compromised slightly on middle series and the very best on later series. Garbell knows absolutely nothing about the F-86 development history. Stability and control, manoeuvrability and take off characteristics were defined in a specification R-1815A and B and were in widespread use by the time of the F-86 design. This specification was developed to use concrete data in place of pilot 'sweet' comments and rumours such as Garbell's. Nowhere in his disposition does Garbell mention R-1815 or its later version, 8785, in effect today.

Findings

Findings of the accident investigation

1. The aircraft was certified in accordance with existing regulations

2. The pilot was certified and held a valid letter of authority for the flight.

3. The regulations and procedures concerning certification of experimental aircraft, and issuance of letters of authority for pilots were inadequate.

4. The aircraft was capable of taking off from Runway 30 without incident under the conditions at Sacramento.

5. The differences between the horizon and runway length at Oakland and Sacramento created visual illusions that induced an apparent need for rapid lift off at Sacramento (Ed Horkey's note: Only for Bingham. It is interesting to note that a section of the report reads "a second, and perhaps more significant factor is the previously mentioned visual cues. The pilot was accustomed to establishing a takeoff attitude by reference to the environment around runway 29 at Oakland, where the 'wide open' expanse of San Francisco bay creates a very definite horizon. This results in the visual impression of an "unlimited" runway. Actually the horizon would appear to recede as the aircraft moved along the runway. Under these circumstances takeoffs by the inexperienced pilot were accomplished with little likelihood of overrotation. Although the pilot established a takeoff attitude by reference to the amount of runway remaining the actual lift off attitude would be tempered by the length of the runway and the sensory illusion that the end of the runway was still quite distant."

6. The pilot did not have sufficient experience in the Sabre Mk 5 to enable him to compensate for the misleading visual clues.

7. The catastrophic consequence of this accident is directly attributed to the proximity of the shopping center to the runway.

Probable cause listed by NTSB:

The National Transportation Safety Board determines that the probable cause of this accident was the overrotation of the aircraft and subsequent derogation of the performance capability. The overrotation was the result of inadequate pilot proficiency in the aircraft and misleading visual clues.

As soon as the USAF received its first F-86A Sabres in 1949 it soon found formation flying easy, with good thrust-to-weight ratio, a stable airframe and the reliable General Electric J-47 engine. Immediately the first Sabre aerobatic team was formed at Langley Air Force Base, Virginia. The team comprised five F-86As from the 4th Fighter Interceptor Group, 335 FS and was led by Captain Vermont Garrison. Named *The Silver Sabres* the aircraft used comprised 48-233, '244, '262, '273, '293 and '294. As their name implies the aircraft were natural metal with the fuselage motif of an Indian Chief's head mounted on a flaming arrow. This was the only Sabre team known to exist prior to the outbreak of the Korean war.

Several other USAF units flew Sabre aerobatic teams during the 1950s including the 94th FS at Oxnard AFB, California which had a team of four F-86As called the *Sabre Dancers* in 1954.

One of the better known teams flying Sabres was the *Sabre Knights* from the 325 Fighter Interceptor Squadron at Hamilton AFB, California. This team of four F-86Fs was formed in August 1952 by Major Vince Gordon, who previously led the *Skyblazers* in Europe. The aircraft wore red and yellow striped fins and nose trim. Serial numbers were 51-2751, '842,

'806 and '805. In May 1954, the *Sabre Knights* changed from the F-86F model to the F-86D, their first display with the new variant being at Hamilton AFB on 15th May 1954. They flew a 20 minute show at venues in California and surrounding States until they disbanded at the end of the 1955 season. F-86Ds used by the team included 52-3678, '730, '692 and '697. USAF Sabres deployed to Europe were soon employed as aerobatic mounts. The USAF were keen to continue the *Skyblazers* team which had been flying F-84E Thunderjets until July 1953. The 48th Fighter Wing at Chaumont, France, began to convert to the F-86F Sabre early in 1953 and reformed the *Skyblazers* in July 1954, with four Sabres in red, white and blue trim. The first colour scheme included the tail surfaces and outer wing panels being painted with large areas of red and white, with various sized medium blue stars in the white areas. Led by Major William N. Dillard, the *Skyblazers* continued in this form throughout 1955, then changed the colour scheme for the 1956 season to include white stars on blue tail surfaces and outer wing panels.

The *Skyblazers* legend was painted in Old English style red script on both sides of the fuselage. The Statue of Liberty badge also appeared on both sides of the fuselage. The team gave their last display with F model

Sabres in October 1956 before converting to the F-100C Super Sabre. The aircraft used included 53-1192, 53-1162, 53-1186 and 53-1201.

Even the USAF's Air National Guard formed Sabre aerobatic teams at an early stage. In 1957, the Colorado Air National Guard re-equipped from the F-80C Shooting Star to the F-86F Sabre. They operated an aerobatic team

F-86
Aerobatic Teams
The History of the world's Sabre Teams

Adrian Balch details the use of the Sabre and its variants as a leading mount for some of the world's most famous aerial artists

with the former type called the *Minute Men* so the Sabre was an obvious choice for the new mount. As this team came from an Air National Guard the pilots were all part time, having civilian jobs during the week. With their new mounts the *Minute Men* staged the first jet precision demonstration ever held in Hawaii, in April 1957. Their 25 minute display was highlighted by 20 minutes of smoke trails. It was the first team to carry enough smoke so that it could be used throughout the entire show. Other teams with Sabres only carried about three minutes supply. Apparently the team claimed they could lay a trail of smoke from Montreal to Miami. During 1958 the team claimed to be the first to do five ship rolls and loops in the USA. It was also the first team to do the low-altitude corkscrew manoeuvre in which the two wing aircraft simultaneously did rolls around the leader and tail aircraft, forming spiral smoke trails in the air.

During their period of operation the *Minute Men* only had one accident. This was on June 7th 1958 when Captain John T. Ferrier was killed during an air show at Patterson Air Force

Base, Ohio. Rather than eject from his Sabre Captain Ferrier guided his ill-fated aircraft away from a densely populated area and crashed on open ground. The team was lead by Colonel Walter Williams until March 1959 when Captain Bob Cherry took over as leader. The team took

Top Left: Colorado Air National F-86F of The Minute Men in 1957/58 (Colorado ANG). Above: Members of the Skyblazers aerial demonstration team stand in front of one of their F-86 aircraft at Chaumont Air Base, France on 24th March 1956 (USAF Photo). Below: Four F-86Es of the Italian Air Force Cavallino Rampante in 1956

six F-86F Sabres, including a spare, around to air shows accompanied by a T-33 support ship. They continued operations until the close of the 1959 show season, then disbanded. Colour scheme was natural metal with red fuselage top, fin, undersides of the fuselage, wings and tailplanes. *Minute Men* appeared in red script along the fuselage sides. F-86Fs operated by the team were 51-2826, '867, ' 868,'855, '884, and '900.

Under the Mutual Defense Assistance program, the United States provided a number of nations with various marks of the Sabre. A number were also manufactured by other nations namely Canada, Italy, Japan and Australia.

Some twenty air forces received Sabres from one of these sources and, on seeing the success of the USAF aerobatic teams were eager to share the prestige and publicity that the Sabre had brought them. Nearly every country that procured the type formed an aerobatic team with them, giving testimony to the aircraft's design and reliability. Canadair built over 1000 Sabres, re-engined with the Orenda, while the Australian Commonwealth Aircraft Corporation Pty. modified the fuselage to take the Rolls-Royce Avon powerplant. These engine changes seemed to make little difference to aerobatic team eligibility as all variants performed with teams apart from the H, K and L models.

The Royal Canadian Air Force's first team formed in 1954, named the *Prarie Pacific Team* at Cold Lake, Alberta. Simultaneously, the *Fireballs* were formed in Europe at Soellingen, Germany with four red painted Sabres from No. 3 Fighter Wing. The following year, No. 1 Air Division, N0. 2 Fighter Wing formed the *Sky*

Lancers at Grosentquin, France. They participated in many International Air shows throughout Europe in 1955, including one of West Germany's first air shows following the lifting of the post-war ban on aviation in that country. The most famous RCAF team, and one of the most famous Sabre teams overall, was the *Golden Hawks* which formed with six Canadair Sabre Mk. 5s in 1959 to help celebrate the RCAF's 35th anniversary and the 50th Anniversary of Flight in Canada. Giving shows throughout Canada and the United States the teams final year was 1963. Their 317th and final show was staged at Montreal. Although training for another season began the RCAF disbanded the team on 28th February 1964. Painted Gold overall the smart scheme featured a red and white fuselage cheat line with a hawks head design. *Golden Hawks* Sabres included 23066, 23073, 23164, 23424, 23457, 23487, 23649 and 23651.

Across the other side of the world, Taiwan's Chinese Nationalist Air Force had received a very large supply of Sabres, taking on charge many that had fought in Korea as well as newer models.

Surprisingly, even the Chinese formed Sabre aerobatic team called the *Thunder Tigers*. This team had already been operating F-84G Thunderjets and in 1959 converted to the F-86F Sabre, increasing the number in the team from nine to twelve. They demonstrated their skills throughout Taiwan, Korea, Okinawa and the Philippines as well as in Thailand where they performed before the Thai Royal Family. The *Thunder Tigers* finally relinquished its Sabres in 1967 when they re-equipped with the Northrop F-5A. *Thunder Tigers* Sabres were natural metal overall with a red or dark blue

Top: *The first Sabre aerobatic team was the Silver Sabres flying F-86As from 335FS, 4th Fighter Group in 1949/50. This particular aircraft is an F-86A-5NA, 48-273. The aircraft looks almost brand new - straight out of the factory. (Photo via David Menard)*

nose design and a black/yellow chequered sash around the fuselage. Their aircraft included 373/51-13387, 430/55-5009, 392/52-5525 and 265/52-4438.

In Europe, Greece had also received a number of Canadair built F-86E Sabres and started aerobatic training in September 1957 at Tanagra Air Base. Initially using five aircraft, the team later increased to seven and was operated by the 341 Interception Squadron which was part of 114 Combat Wing. Named the *Hellenic Flame*, this team made their first official appearance in May 1958 and gave shows in Greece, Italy, France and West Germany. In 1961 the team relocated to the airport of Anghialos and gave many more shows in the following years, including participating in the 1963 Paris Air Show followed by displays in Italy and Turkey. 1964 was the final year for the team. After six years of operations and several awards and decorations *Hellenic Flame*, disbanded in September 1964. Colour scheme was blue and white upper surfaces with orange undersides. Serials of team aircraft included 19294, '377, '382, '392, and '448. Among other Sabre users was Iran which re-equipped its *Golden Crown* aerobatic team from F-84G Thunderjets to F-86F Sabres in 1960. These lasted until 1967 when they were replaced by F-5A Freedom Fighters.

Italy was a prolific user of the Sabre in its aerobatic teams with no less than three taking up the Canadair built aircraft as its mount. The rst of these was *Cavalliono Rampante* (Rampant Horses) from 4 Aerobrigata at Pratica di Mare. Flying four aircraft painted primrose yellow with red nose trim and blue tails and wingtips surmounted by white stars, the team formed in 1956 for the Paris Air Show disbanding at the end of the following year. The next Sabre team was the black painted *Lanceri Neri* (Black Lancers) from 2 Aerobrigata at Cameri. With red/white/green national colours under the wings this team of six aircraft formed in 1958 and participated in air shows in Italy, England, France, Germany and Persia (now Iran), disbanding at the end of 1959.

The third, and most famous team to operate the Sabre in Italy was *Frecce Tricolori* (Tri-coloured Arrows) who were formed on the type early in 1961, operating nine Canadair F-86E Sabres painted black overall with a pale blue diamond design on the fuselage and red/white/green stripes under the wings and tailplanes. Led by Major M. Scala who was succeeded by Major M. Squarcina in October 1961, the Sabres retained this colour scheme until 1963 when they adopted the overall dark blue scheme with the Tri-coloured arrows insignia down the fuselage sides as applied later to their Fiat G.91PANs. Appearing at venues Europe-wide these included the 1963 Paris Air Show which was their last year of operations with the Sabre before re-equipping with the Fiat G-91 for the following season.

Canadair also delivered 34 Sabres to South Africa, who formed two lesser known squadron teams during the late 1960s. In Japan, Mitsubishi assembled 300 F-86F Sabres at Nagoya. The last of these, in February 1961, was the last Sabre to be manufactured. Consequently, the Japanese Air Self Defense Force was one of the last air arms to operate the Sabre. In the Spring of 1958 it was decided to form full time aerobatic team to represent the JASDF at shows and events throughout Japan for recruiting and public relations. Preparatory studies were started and conducted by four instructors on F-86F Sabres at Hamamatsu Air Base. In the Spring of 1960 the *Blue Impulse* Aerobatic Team was formed and gave their first public demonstration on 4th March that year. Five F-86F Sabres were used of which one flew solo demonstrations while the main formation regrouped. Initially, the Sabres retained their natural metal finish overall, with the Wing's black and yellow chequered band across the fin. The following year, 1961, the aircraft were painted in their own colour scheme which was still basically natural metal but with blue and white trim. The Leader's aircraft had the same scheme but with a gold and white trim. This scheme was retained for two years until 1963, when the second and final colour scheme was implemented. The aircraft were basically white overall apart from the underside of the wings. Trim was medium blue with orange-red trim on the under surfaces. This colourful scheme was retained right up until the F-86F was retired in 1981. If that wasn't attractive enough, the *Blue Impulse*

team used blue, pink, white, yellow and green smoke during their display - a different colour for each of the five aircraft. In 1964, japan was the host for the Olympic games. The *Blue Impulse* team opened the games by making the famous Olympic rings symbol in smoke over the stadium. Five Sabres flew a ring each with a diameter of 6000 feet and 1000 feet separation between each ring. A similar, but more intricate exercise was performed in 1970, when Tokyo hosted EXPO 70. Through a complicated series of well-planned manoeuvres the five Sabres wrote EXPO 70 in white smoke over Tokyo. These were just two highlights in over twenty years of safe operations with the F-86F Sabres. The *Blue Impulse* team flew final demonstrations with their Sabres during the morning and afternoon of 8th February 1981 over Iruma Air Base near Tokyo. In the 21 years of operating the F-86 *Blue Impulse* Sabres flew 545 performances before disbanding prior to re-equipping with their current mount, Mitsubishi T-2 Trainers. Over the 21 year period some 40 Sabres were painted in *Blue Impulse* markings.

One part time team worthy of mention were

the *Flying Jokers* operated by 332 Squadron of the Royal Norwegian Air Force. In May 1957, this team re-equipped from the F-84G Thunderjet to the F-86 Sabre, increasing the teams number from five to six. The *Flying Jokers* were the first team to fly Card Five formation and disbanded in the Autumn of 1964, when their aircraft were transferred to 334 Squadron.

Before the Royal Air Force *Black Arrows* looped 22 Hunters at Farnborough in September 1958, the Pakistan Air Force held the record for looping the largest number of aircraft in formation. Sixteen F-86F Sabres were looped in perfect diamond formation on 2nd February 1958 at a huge air display at Karachi. This historic loop was performed by *The Falcons* who displayed this feat before the King of Afghanistan and the Chiefs of Staff of the Turkish, Iranian, Jordanian and Afghanistan Air Forces. Led by Wing

Top: *The RCAF Golden Hawks Sabres had number codes on their fins for a time. Here is 23651, the Leader's aircraft. (Werner Gysin).* **Below:** *Sabres of the Royal Hellenic Air Force aerobatic team lined up at Le Bourget during the 1963 Paris Air Show. Nearest aircraft is '448' (Werner Gysin).*

F-86 Aerobatic Teams

Commander M.Z. Masud, the pilots were drawn from 11, 15, 5 and 4 Squadrons. *The Falcons* were formed in 1956 by 11 Squadron as a four man team, increasing to seven the following year. At the time they were thought to have the largest number of jet aircraft in an aerobatic team worldwide. However, not content with this they gradually increased the number until they had 16 Sabres,. After its sixteen aircraft display in 1958, the *The Falcons* reverted to a four member team for several years. In 1963, No. 11 Squadron moved to Sargodha when they increased their number to nine and were led by Wing Commander Anwar Shamin. Following a display at Peshawar in 1964 the team disbanded.

Another Far Eastern Sabre equipped country was the Philippines, which received their F-86Fs in 1957 and immediately formed *The Blue Diamonds* team with seven aircraft. Shows were flown throughout the Philippines until the team reequipped with the F-5A in 1968.

Other countries that operated Sabres in the aerobatic team role included Portugal, South Africa, Argentine (*Southern Cross Aerobatic Flight*), Spain (*Arrowheads*), and Turkey (*White Swans*).

The Royal Australian Air Force, operating CAC built Avon powered aircraft from 1954 operated several aerobatic teams. The first of these to be formed was *The Black Diamonds* from 75 Squadron. This team was formed on the 40th Anniversary of the RAAF in 1961 and their Sabres were fitted with smoke making equipment. This for three years before disbanding in 1964. The second Sabre aerobatic team was operated by 76 Squadron at RAAF Williamtown, N.S.W. and was called *The Black Panthers*. They were operational in 1962, the aircraft sporting a large Panther insignia on the fuselage. The following year 76 Squadron replaced this team with another, calling themselves *The Red Diamonds* - naturally a large red diamond and lightning flash replaced the Panther insignia. The RAAF were represented in the Far East by No. 3 Squadron's team of Sabres at Butterworth, Malaysia during 1966, but it wasn't until 1968 that the RAAF formed another team called *The Marksmen* - operated by No. 2 OCU at Williamtown. With yellow and black striped fins these Sabres were also equipped to make smoke and brought the RAAF Sabre aerobatics team era to a close when they disbanded at the end of 1968.

This is then a round up of most of the better known aerobatic teams that have operated the Sabre worldwide. This closes yet another chapter in the story of a famous and classic jet fighter. WW Adrian Balch.

Top: The Blue Impulse operated this F-86F serial 62-7501 seen here at Iruma on November 3rd 1980 *Above:* The Frecce Tricolori Sabres in their second colour scheme, photographe late in 1963 after the tail codes were changed from letters to numbers (Italian Air Forc Photograph).*Right:* This preserved F-86E is painted in the colours of Cavilono Rampani and is based at Rivolto, 12th May 1983.

Top: *This North American FJ-4 Fury, Bu N 139486 is preserved at the Naval Air Museum Pensacola, Florida in the colours of Nav Attack Unit VA-192. (MAP via Dunca Curtis)* **Right below:** *Looking more like Sabre once off the ground and with its unde carriage retracted this gate guard FJ version is Bu No 141376 and is preserved Beaufort MCAS - shown here in 1981 (MAI*

Designated model NA-134 (FJ-1 Fury) and NA-181(FJ-2 Fury) the aircraft was a derivative of the USAF's swept wing F-86. Many view it as the equivalent of the F-86E with the incorporation of a lengthened front strut on the landing gear for flight deck operation and the addition of catapult and arrestor hooks for launching and recovery from aircraft carriers. Though the FJ-1 variant had not been viewed as a success by the U.S. Navy, procurement executives monitored the success of the F-86 in Korea and came to the conclusion that the best way to acquire a good fighter bomber in a relatively short time was to order an essentially navalised version of the Sabre.

Two XFJ-2 prototypes were ordered on 8th March 1951 - basically two modified F-86Es - as well as an XFJ-2B which was armed with four 20mm cannons in place of the six .50in machine guns carried by the F-86. Robert 'Bob' Hoover flew the XFJ-2B for the first time on 27th December 1951 with the basic XFJ-2 flying the following February. Both aircraft were immediately delivered to the United States Navy for aerial trials and a carrier evaluation was conducted aboard the USS *Coral Sea* in December 1952. The trails were heralded as a success. By February 1952 the U.S.N. had placed an order for 300 FJ-2s which were named Fury. Production was launched at the Columbus, Ohio factory and the first produc-

Paul Coggan examines the story behind the North American Aviation FJ Fury series aircraft - not a Sabre, but a very close relative!

tion FJ-2 was to take to the air in October 1952. Essentially it incorporated all the refinements of the successful F-86F model with the addition of wider landing gear tyres, fully powered tail surfaces and folding wings. An AN/APG radar was installed as a standard fit. The FJ-2 was armed with four 20mm cannons and powered by the J47-GE-2.

Due to the Korean War, production priority at Columbus dictated the F-86 be pushed ahead of the FJ-2 programme and as a result only 25 FJ-2s were delivered to the Navy by the close of 1953. As a result the production order was reduced to 200 airframes, the last FJ-2s leaving the production lines as late as September 1954.

The early FJ-2s were considered less than suitable for carrier based operations and as a result the aircraft were diverted to the U.S. Marine Corps.

The 18th April 1952 had seen a twist in the

story with the U.S. Navy placing a further orde for a new, Wright J-65-W-2 powered versio (the Wright powerplant was a licence bui British Armstrong-Siddeley *Sapphire* engine) the Fury designated FJ-3. The more powerfu FJ-3 first flew on 11th December 1953, bein followed by more than 450 airframes in th same production run.

The more powerful FJ-3 was looked upo favourably by the U.S. Navy who equippe some 18 Fighter Squadrons with the aircraf In addition two new Marine Corps units wer allocated FJ-3s, and the earlier FJ-2 equippe units, of which there were now four, were re equipped with the type.

As the new dash 3 Furies were being presse into service, the North American design tea were already beavering away at the developmen of the next in the line fighter, the FJ-4. B increasing the internal fuel capacity by 50% and modification of the entire airframe wit refinements in the fuselage and mainplan area the aircraft maintained its performanc standards but had an increased range.

North American Aviation's

FABULOUS
FJ FURY

The newly configured FJ-4 prototype flew for the first time on 28th October 1954 with Test Pilot Richard Wenzell at the controls. Despite the fact the aircraft still carried the same basic designation it was a very different animal. The Columbus production line of North American Aviation rolled out some 150 FJ-4s between early 1955 and early April 1957, all of these airframes being assigned to three U.S.M.C. units. The final version of the Fury was the FJ-4B, of which the aircraft that is the subject of the following feature is one. Effectively an F-86H with additional hardpoints for external stores, and a nuclear weapons carrying capacity, the FJ-4B also had the capability to carry air to surface Bullpup missiles. The wing structure had also been reinforced to support the additional load carrying capabilities. 222 airframes were produced, all for delivery to front line U.S. Navy and U.S. Marine Corps squadrons. The first FJ-3 flew on 3rd December 1956 with the last delivery being made in 1958. **WW PAC**

Top: *Also preserved at Pensacola in U.S. Navy midnight blue colours this shapely Fury is a dash 3 version in the colours of VF-51. The more powerful FJ-3 first flew on 11th December 1953, being followed by more than 450 airframes in the same production run. The type was looked upon favourably by the U.S. Navy who equipped some 18 Fighter Squadrons with the aircraft. In addition two new Marine Corps units were allocated FJ-3s (MAP Via Duncan Curtis)*

Larry Mockford's FANTASTIC FURY

Skip Stagg interviews Larry Mockford about his unique North American FJ-4B and ex N.A.A. Test Pilot Ed Gillespie who relates some interesting facts about the type

Canadian businessman Larry Mockford is the owner of and the energy behind T-Bird Aviation. I was invited to watch whilst Larry put the finishing touches to his latest project, an ex Flight Systems Canadair Silver Star Mk. III. After completing the last phase of flight testing the aircraft was to be flown to Pocatello, Idaho for painting.

Larry then introduced me to his next project, a very interesting, unique and exciting fighter based endeavour. At first glance the aircraft appeared to be the famous F-86 but closer inspection revealed the canopy lines and engine intake to be strikingly different. "It's an FJ Fury" Larry proudly declared, "and it will undergo restoration this winter."

The once proud fighter looked rather neglected though most certainly complete. However, I was assured that under the care of T-Bird Aviation the Fury will be turning heads at next years airshows. Larry acquired the aircraft in 1991 from Flight Systems. They had stored it in the Mojave desert for the past twelve years.

Manufactured by North American Aviation at their Columbus, Ohio plant in 1958, FJ-4B Bu 143575 (c/n 244-83) carries the FAA registration N400FS, for Flight Systems as the aircraft was once owned by them. When Flight Systems acquired the aircraft in 1971 it had only 761 hours on the airframe. After service in the flight test and research duties it undertook with Flight Systems the total time is now 1468 hours.

During inspection of the airframe I was lucky to be introduced to Mr. Ed Gillespie. Ed will probably be performing some of the test flying

for Larry when the aircraft is complete. Ed ha significant connections with the type, havin served as a test pilot at North America Aviation in the 1950s. He certainly had som interesting facts and stories to relay about th type.

Ed reflected on the 20mm cannons installe in the FJ-4B, having fired them from Banshee in anger during the Korean conflict. "For som stupid reason," Ed explained, "the guns on th FJ-3 series were incorrectly mounted." The were installed facing downward with respect t the aircraft's ARL, or aircraft reference line. " anything, you would want them elevate allowing you to lead your target in a dog-figh This made for lousy air to air gunnery work Ed commented. Only a few pilots could ma: ter the misaligned guns. However, the gu problem was corrected in the field at th request of Navy and Marine pilots and follow ing this the Fury gained the respect of the pilo that flew it. Ed continued to debate the attri utes of the 20mm cannons and the MiGs fought against. "The MiGs would take a lot hits from the .50 cal the Air Force was st employing on their F-86s, but one hit from 20mm High explosive incendiary round wou do sufficient damage to a MiG and take it ou of action." Ed felt that if the USAF ha employed 20mm cannons like the Navy the MiG kill ratio would have been much higher.

As Ed was involved in the flight testing of th Fury at North American Aviation I asked if h had any experience with the rocket assiste version of the aircraft. He did, and provide me with an insight to the test phase and pe formance of the FJ-4F series as the rock assisted aircraft were known. The rocket sy: tem, known as the AR-2, produced some 600 pounds of thrust when ignited. The AR-2 wa mounted just above the jet exhaust ar employed either a monopropellant or a bipr pellant depending on the test being conducte at the time.

Hydrogen Peroxide was employed in inte nally mounted stainless steel tanks, and mixe with JP-4 to provide quite a potent cocktail f

e AR-2. Normal test profile was to be in level ght at 42,000 feet at maximum jet thrust nen the AR-2 was ignited. Ed described the xperience as " a real kick in the seat" when e rocket came to life. A climb to 70,000 feet as not unusual in the flight profile.

Ed, like many other test pilots, as not npressed with the altitudes reached by the rcraft. He explained his main concern was to ep the rocket from exploding. The flight test- g was conducted with one eye fixed on the ydrogen Peroxide tank pressure gauge. Under ormal conditions, with the rocket running, the nk would show a decrease in pressure as the eroxide was consumed. However, with a fire, nich occurred several times Ed recalled, the mergency procedure was to dump the rocket el and continue running the rocket at max

I could have seen his expression when I lit off the rocket. On that flight I indicated 1.42 Mach in level flight at 42,000 feet! The sight of the mis-identified F-86 disappearing over the horizon provided a lost of grist for the story mill at the officers club that night," Ed reminisced.

And what of the flight handling qualities? "The Marines really loved the aircraft......it was a good high altitude attacker. " He went on to say that the aircraft offered good ground support capabilities from its ability to carry and deliver large amounts of ordnance. No difficulties were reported with carrier operations. The high pressure tyres (main gear was at 150psi and nose wheel at 200psi) along with a trailing arm type main landing gear provided for good ground handling qualities and carrier operations.

mounted stores. Ed highlighted how the asymmetrical condition, from having a wing tank and Mark 7 on the left wing and single wing tank on the starboard wing, was overcome. This uneven loading resulted in a slipping condition and was addressed by both lateral and longitudinal trim. The flight controls would allow the pilot to trim the aircraft out of asymmetrical condition.

Ed was directly involved in the spin research at NASA, Langley. He reported that the Fury spun inverted very viciously. While it was difficult to enter an inverted spin, the exit was close to impossible. The final recommended procedure resulting from the investigation was to avoid the condition altogether! Upon entering an unusual condition or altitude, you simply placed all the controls, including the thrust

rust to evacuate as much fuel as possible in e shortest possible time. An increase in tank essure would indicate the emergency proce- re was not working and an explosion was minent. The procedure at this point was to il out! Considering the altitudes and air- eed at which the aircraft was operating this s not a very attractive alternative. As for the speed attained with the rocket system, Ed iiled and remembered one flight as he was turning to the Columbus plant airfield. As s often the case, an Air Force interceptor uld challenge a Marine or Navy fighter at h altitude. The challenge was duly offered an F-94F, a very hot radar interceptor of the y. ".......he was off my right wing going in and t of afterburner trying to get me to engage. eally didn't have time to play as I was con- cting a flight test and keeping one eye on e Hydrogen Peroxide pressure gauge. I wish

Early versions of the Fury had problems with flutter at high speed flight, Ed disclosed. However, the addition of high aspect ratio stabilators and a split rudder system solved the problem. Ed pointed out the spoilers mounted on the flaps. The spoilers allowed the Fury to handle crosswind landings very well. The flaps were equipped with what was referred to as gipper doors. Mounted along the underside leading edge of the flaps, these doors would extend and provide limited boundary control to what would normally be a simple slotted flap system.

All of what would now be called contemporary control services and the addition of leading edge devices on the main wing contributed to the superior handling qualities of the aircraft.

This superior handling quality was further emphasised by Ed when he discussed the wing

Left Lower: Larry Mockford and the Wright J-65 powerplant - a licence built version of the Sapphire jet engine. Above. November 400FS has been stored in the Mojave desert in California for a number of years. The Flight Systems company logo is visible in this photograph (All photo's via the author)

lever, to the central position. The aircraft would recover to a diving spiral, where recovery by the pilot was less terrifying and demanding.

Furies employed speed brakes, not unlike the F-86, which are mounted in an equivalent location and open forward to provide similar function. However, the Fury also employed two additional speed brakes further aft of the F-86 style units. These two larger speed brakes, working in conjunction with the forward speed brakes, allowed the Fury to perform a vertical delivery of ordnance. When opened, Ed stated the aircraft would experience only minor pitch-

Above: Close up of the much modified nose strut on the FJ-4B Fury. Basically a Navalised F-86H the FJ-4B had a longer, stronger nose wheel strut and oleo to enable the type to operate from aircraft carriers without problem. High pressure tyres were also used all round. Right: Close up of the starboard nose section. Below: The FJ-4B in the open hangar at Mojave. This shot shows the higher angle of attack of the Naval fighter and emphasises the compactness of the type.

ing and slow the aircraft enormously, a distinct advantage when dog-fighting. he further described the Fury as bristling like a porcupine when the speed brakes were deployed!

This attribute is also reported as being employed by one of the *Flight Systems* pilots, Mr. Tom Armstrong, during development flying for the Pershing missile seeker. Records indicate that N400FS, equipped with the Pershing equipment, would climb to 50,000 feet, enter a vertical dive and recover at 7000

feet. This manoeuvre was conducted several times a day over an eight month period. Clearly, both Mr. Armstrong and the aircraft earned their pay!

One of Larry Mockford's primary concerns during the restoration project will be the close inspection of the larger aft speed brakes. The dynamic loads experienced during the Pershing missile seeker development testing may have caused stress damage to the empennage of the airframe. So, with all these documented advantages what was the underlying cause for the Fury failing as a fighter? Ed responds "For the price of three Furies the Navy could obtain four A-4 Skyhawks. It was like comparing a Cadillac to a Volkswagen, and the Fury was the Cadillac."

Miscellany
Curiously, all referenced airspeeds for gear operation, flap retraction along with canopy

closure are all the same - 235 knots. While the recommended speeds for base leg of 130 knots and final approach, 125 knots, are important the aircraft was flown by reference to angle o attack. Due to the variations in operating weight, the aircraft was equipped with an angle of attack indicator which would provide the pilot with a safe operating profile.

On a side note, the reason for the high oper ating airspeed for the canopy, 235 knots, is fo pilot safety. While the Furies were equipped with ejection seats, they did not have the zero/zero ejection capabilities that today's jet enjoy. It was felt that having an open canopy would allow the pilot the chance to escape from the aircraft should the 'Carriers catapul (called the shot, or taking the shot) fail to launch the aircraft successfully.

Weapons
In addition to the four Mk. 12 20 mm cannon

op: As the Fury is a rare piece of U.S. Naval ad American aviation history Larry ockford wants to see the aircraft rebuilt and t back in the air. When the restoration is mplete it will be the only operational FJ-4B ury in existence.

ne Fury was also equipped to deliver a Mk.7 iclear weapon. The delivery method was nown as a LABS delivery. The Mk.7 was ounted on the left wing centre section on a IcLaren rack, an electrical ejectable rack, board of the left 200 gallon external wing nk.

LABS delivery required the fighter to be in vel flight at 45,000 feet moving as fast as pos- ble, then to enter a zoom type climb. At a redetermined position the weapon would be leased in a loft trajectory toward the target. Whilst the concept of loft delivery is sound, le possibility of escaping the resulting estruction of the target was always in ques- ons by the pilots who conducted the mission. he turning abilities of a fighter, at the final fting altitude and airspeed, was not sufficient escape the area. Fortunately, this subject ill always remain in debate as the delivery of iclear weapons was never necessary.

To support the Fury in this mission, a buddy inker concept was developed. The buddy inker consisted of a Fury equipped with a 400 allon external in-flight refuelling system. The xternal buddy tank was also fitted with a rogue basket to interface with the Fury's wing ounted refuelling probe. The basket drogue buld be identified at night by a series of glow- g buttons. This identification system, ombined with an unlit wing probe produced system that was at best very poor. The mis- on of the buddy tanker was to escort the trike Fury as far into the mission as possible. hen, at 45,000 feet the escorting Fury would ansfer all its fuel in the internal and external ores, including its own 200 gallon wing tanks,

to the Strike Fury. This procedure would allow the Fury tanker just enough fuel to return to the nearest friendly base.

The Restoration

As the Fury is a rare piece of U.S. Naval and American aviation history Larry Mockford wants to see the aircraft rebuilt and put back in the air. When the restoration is complete it will be the only operational FJ-4B Fury in existence. However, business is business, and at the time of writing T-B*ird* A*viation* are currently working with several parties to establish both the cost of restoration and how the aircraft can be employed to earn its keep afterwards. Parties in the airshow business along with

Below: The existing cockpit flight instru- ments inside N400FS. Someone was very concerned about aircraft heading!

research and development companies have expressed interest in the aircraft's capabilities. One thing is for certain - the aircraft will not be going back to *Flight Systems*, and it will not leave the United States. Nor will it be cut up for scrap!

Furies were perhaps one of the first fighter aircraft to benefit from advanced manufacturing technologies. A chemical milling procedure was employed to produce the Fury's wet wing fuel tanks. To assemble the wing section a special sealant was developed. Ed speculated that *T-Bird Aviation's* Fury may experience some fuel streaking from the wings during the first few hours of flight testing. He expressed that this was normal following long term storage and that the streaking would subside. Normally, when an aircraft is placed in long term storage at Mojave the tanks are filled with jet fuel. As this was the case with N400FS, the wet wing fuel tanks should have survived the protracted storage in the open.

When the aircraft was in military service, it employed a liquid oxygen or LOX system to supply breathing oxygen to the pilot. A close inspection of the forward nose section revealed that the Lox system was replaced, presumably while in service at *Flight Systems*, with a standard high pressure oxygen tank. The employment of such a standard oxygen system will aid the restoration as it is a simple 'plumbing' problem.

The normal empty weight of N400FS is

13,000lbs. Maximum gross take off weight is 26,000lbs. For reference the gross weight of a T-33 Mk II is 15,500lbs. Furies are not light weight fighters!

An update on the Fury restoration project by T-Bird Aviation.

On a recent visit to Mojave airport I checked on Larry Mockford's T-*Bird Aviation's* Fury restoration efforts.

The Fury was not in residence in Larry's hangar. I feared that the aircraft had not survived its extended storage in the desert, or that major damage was discovered in the airframe,

Top: *The three main forces behind th rebuild, to flying condition, of the uniqu North American FJ-4B Fury N400FS - Sco McDonnell, Hall Bells and Larry Mockford*

rendering the restoration project financiall unachievable.

Larry informed me that the Fury was move to *Tracor's* maintenance hangar where it wa undergoing disassembly and detailed inspec tion.

After spending $2,500.00 for hydraulic hose and additional funds on labour and hanga space, Larry is committed to the restoration c this aircraft. Complete replacement of a

hydraulic hoses was necessary to bring the systems up to standards and specifications.

The landing gear has undergone several gear retraction cycles with power supplied from a hydraulic mule or pump. The remaining hydraulic systems and flight controls have had the system pressure taken to 3000 psi, which is normal for this aircraft. No leaks or problems have presented themselves during the pressure tests. Additionally, the canopy was removed to make a cast for a new one at a local custom shop.

While shooting the photographs for the follow up story I was surprised to learn of another advanced feature of this aircraft. A Ram Air Turbine, or RAT, is pictured (above, second hatch back from front) in its operational or deployed mode on the right side of the aircraft. The purpose of a RAT is to provide back up hydraulic power to the flight controls during engine failure. As Tracor's mechanic, Hall Bells, stated, "It allows you to fly to a better place before you have to bail out."

The fuel system was pressure checked and is in great shape. As the Fury was in long term storage in the desert and exposed to the elements, there was concern regarding the condition of the fuel system. The jet fuel placed in the tanks prior to the Fury being put in storage twelve years ago did its job and preserved the system.

The wet wing tanks are the same construction as the Rockwell Sabreliners' (SABRE-40). A sealant chamber along the underside of the leading edge of the wing allows the sealant to be replaced or repaired as necessary.

The aircraft is in better condition than Larry of Tracor's Mr. Bells expected. The Fury is in good hands at the moment as Mr. Bells was the last mechanic on the aircraft when the Fury was owned by Flight Systems. Additionally, Mr.Bells was with the aircraft in the field when it was used as a test bed for the Pershing missile seeker programme.

Mr.Scott McDonnell, who is also experienced in working this Fury and is Tracor's "chief wrench bender," expressed surprise on how well the aircraft has been preserved.

Originally, the tail section was to undergo close inspection. The loads experienced during the Pershing missile seeker tests may have induced fatigue loads and stress cracks on the aircraft's empennage. It would appear the aft section now on the aircraft is not the one used during the seeker test. "This is a new aft section and was placed on the aircraft prior to entering storage." stated Mr. Bells. While it will undergo close scrutiny, preliminary inspection indicates a low time tail section.

It is fortunate the aircraft is so well preserved and that Larry has acquired a good supply of parts. The current problem is trying to obtain small parts and seals without having to have them custom made. Larry showed me several small seals that are employed on the single point refuelling system. While there is no problem that money cannot solve, it is small parts and pieces like this that can cause expensive problems and delays on restoration projects.

Mr.Bells stated the only remaining supply of spare parts are from Furies on static displays in museums or as monuments and gate guards.

As to just how many Furies are in existence is now in question.(See our survivors listing on page 67 - Ed) Several Furies that were operated by the U.S. Navy were used as hot fire trainers for crash and rescue personnel and no longer exist.

There is one Fury on display at the Naval Aviation Museum in Pensacola, Florida. Another Fury stands guard at El Toro Marine Airbase in California. As El Toro is now on the list of base closures it is unclear as to what will happen to the aircraft. Other reports indicate as many as 18 to 20 Furies may still exist. But in what condition? Messrs. Mockford, Bells and McDonnell, who make it their business to locate aircraft and parts for restoration projects of this nature, find this estimate of existing aircraft doubtful. What is clear is that this will be the only operational Fury in the world.

Due to the Fury's flight capabilities and the J-65's relatively low operational cost, several contracts are now under negotiation.

Operating cost for the Fury is considerably less than an A-4 and significantly less than an F-4. Low operating cost is an advantage in today's marketplace. It would appear T-Bird Aviation's Fury will be hard work this time next year. Airshows? You bet! **WW Skip Stagg**

China Lake

The

Sabre's
LAST STA

I am pretty sure that no one who witnessed the first flight of the XP-86 in 1947 could have envisaged the distinctive shape of the Sabre still flying in the Californian skies some 45 years later. Even less likely that they would be operated by the U.S. military. But truth is often stranger than fiction, and Sabres do fly on as QF-86s with the U.S. *Naval Air Warfare Center* (NAWC) at China Lake.

The story begins in the late '60s, when personnel at China Lake foresaw that full-size aircraft would be the only realistic targets which could simulate a threat for missile testing. Jay Bornfleth, and others in the Weapons Department soon worked out a means of converting ex military jets into high altitude remotely piloted vehicles, or *Full Scale Aerial Targets* (FSAT) as they became known.

Initially, 32 F-86H Sabres were obtained by the U.S. Navy. These aircraft had been retired by the New York and Maryland Air National Guard, and from 1970, they started a new life with the United States Navy. Many were operated by Navy Squadron VX-4 at Point Mugu Naval Air Station in California. Their relative similarity to the MiG-17 made them an ideal choice as aggressor aircraft in the *Top Gun* programme. However, most of the F-86Hs were converted to drone configuration, and , as QF-86Hs saw service with both *Pacific Missile Test Center* (PMTC) at Point Mugu, and *Naval Weapons Center* China Lake (re-named NAWC on 1st October 1992). QF-86Hs could be flown either 'live' or remotely from a ground station, and most missions were of a non-destructive nature. The last QF-86H was shot down circa 1979.

Obviously, a replacement was badly needed, and what better replacement than a Sabre! In the late '70s, the F-86F was chosen as the next generation FSAT, due to the availability of numerous ex-*Japanese Air Self Defense Force* (JASDF) airframes. As these aircraft had been initially supplied under the U.S. Military Assistance Program, they had to be either scrapped or returned to U.S. control at the end of their service life. Thus, the U.S. navy got their Sabres for merely the cost of disassembly and shipping back to China Lake. Small numbers of F-86Fs were also obtained from Taiwan and the Republic of Korea. Approximately 140 of the best Sabres were earmarked for conversion to QF-86F, and numerous others arrived at China Lake for spares reclamation, including four rare RF-86F Photo reconnaissance aircraft.

Sabres for drone conversion were thoroughly overhauled, and this was where cannibalisation was often resorted to, though masses of spares were also acquired. Only occasionally did a part require manufacturing. Originally, conversion work was done by military person-

Duncan Curtis reports on the use of the Sabre in one of it's last military applications in California, U.S.A. - as a live, full scale target drone and interviews Dick Wright, one of the Sabre pilots.

Top: *The QF-86H can either be flown with a pilot at the controls or, remarkably as a NOLO aircraft (No onboard live operator). A destruct system is fitted to the Sabre in the event that ground control is lost. The black panel fitted to the aircraft has two lights to enable the status of the aircraft to be signalled to a potential piloted escort. Shown here is QF-86F Bu 555072 with Mt. Whitney in the background. The camera used for remote piloting operations can be seen protruding from the radome just above the air intake. The aircraft is seen configured with 2 x 120 drop tanks. (U.S. Navy photograph)* **Left:** *This ex RCAF Mk 5 Sabre (RCAF 23300) is seen here at Mojave on 4th October 1984 registered N4724A (Gerry Manning Collection).*

nel at China Lake, but various civilian contractors were subsequently employed and the NS Division of M*antech* currently carries out drone conversion work at Inyokern Airport, to the west of China Lake. The initial cost of conversion, per aircraft was around $350,000 and this

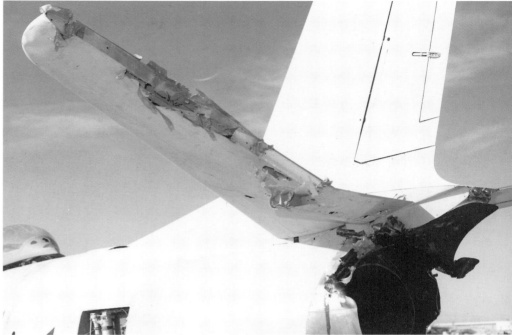

Below: The damage done to QF-86E Bu No 555091 from a heat-seeking Sidewinder missile TM (non-warhead) intercept. The airframe was recovered OK and flew many more times after repair despite the evident damage shown here. Sometimes, the missile will score a direct hit on the Sabre, but since no explosives are fitted the aircraft has a good chance of returning to base. One Sabre drone survived seventeen such missions before being shot down. Currently, NAWC's Sabres are used in numerous U.S. Navy missile programmes, and the majority of their time is spent acting as co-operative targets in the development of F/A-18 Hornet computer software. Nowadays, five lucky people fly the QF-86F at China Lake; three active U.S. Navy pilots, and two civilians.(U.S. Navy Photo)

cluded one or two post conversion test ghts. Like the QF-86H it replaced, the F-86F can be either 'live' piloted, or remotely ontrolled from a ground station. A camera ounted in the nose of the aircraft enables the round operator to monitor the flight via a TV creen. If a remote control or NOLO (No nboard Live Operator) mission is to be flown, destruct system is fitted to the Sabre, in the vent that ground control is lost. A black panel tted to the side of the fuselage has two lights ounted on it, which enables a chase plane lot to see the status of the destruct system; green light indicates 'safe', a red light tells e observer the aircraft is armed. The first F-86F was delivered in 1978, but full missions ere flown starting 1979-80.

Though the QF-86Fs were flown by both PMTC nd NWC, from 1st October 1992 all Sabres ere based at China Lake. All QF-4Ns, drone version of the Phantom II, and successor to the QF-86F, are now single based at Point Mugu. As of late December 1992 there were 15 QF-86Fs remaining in service, sufficient for another year or two's operations.

Currently, NAWC's Sabres are used in numerous U.S. Navy missile programmes, and the majority of their time is spent acting as co-operative targets in the development of F/A-18 Hornet computer software. Nowadays, five lucky people fly the QF-86F at China Lake; three active U.S. Navy pilots, and two civilians. One of these is Dick Wright, who flew big A-5 Vigilantes with the U.S. Navy before he retired 11 years ago. He has been flying Sabres - both live and remote - from China Lake ever since. His thoughts on the Sabre make interesting reading:

"Considering the F-86 design is 45 years old, one of the first swept wing designs, has one of the first mechanical-hydraulic irreversible flight control systems (less the rudder), and was one of the first supersonic airplanes (clean, full power, very high descent rate, at high altitude), it's pretty amazing that it's still flying routinely and safely on a daily basis. It would have been nice to have more thrust (the J-47GE-27 engine puts out about 6000lb thrust), but it's still a delight and enjoyable airplane to fly. It's sad when they're shot down, but if the programme had never gotten started, they probably would have been chopped up for scrap fifteen years ago."

"Fortunately, a great number of spares were available and supply support through the life of the programme has not been a significant problem. Recognising the age of the engines, they are torn down for comprehensive hot section inspection every 1100 flight hours. Generally, our QF-86Fs accumulate 150-250 hours before they are expended. 99% of those flight hours are in the manned configuration."

If missiles are to be fired at a NOLO QF-86F, then a telemetry warhead is usually fitted to enable the maximum data to be collected. Sometimes, the missile will score a direct hit on the Sabre, but since no explosives are fitted the aircraft has a good chance of returning to base. One Sabre drone survived *seventeen* such missions before being shot down. Dick Wright again:

"Flying the FSAT's remotely is not impossible, but it does require the development of some special skills, so it's been productive to have civilians do the job rather than active Navy pilots who would just become proficient, then be transferred. Currently we have four airplanes in flying status, with the remaining airplanes in ready storage. With the relaxation in world tensions, our activity here has begun to ebb. In a year or so, I'll be out on the streets seeking active employment when the last QF-86F succumbs to a missile."

Soon the last Sabre mission will be flown at China Lake, Hopefully, a few Sabres will win a reprieve, and maybe even fly on in safer skies, thanks in part to their long-gone brethren. Maybe Dick Wright won't have to look too hard for another job............WW Duncan Curtis.
Our sincere thanks to Dick Wright for his help in the preparation of this feature

In Pursuit of Perfection
FORT WAYNE'S FIVE

Bob Becker of **Fort Wayne Air Service** tells the story of the pain involved in the rebuilding of the Cavanaugh Flight Museum's Canadair Sabre

Did you ever assemble a large puzzle and end up with one piece missing? What frustration! No doubt we've all experienced it at one time or another. Still, I enjoy building puzzles and I love a good mystery. Many puzzles would be completed and many mysteries solved before a Canadair F-86 Sabre, construction number 1083 would soar again. What follows will be a synopsis of the work entailed to restore the aircraft that would become the *Experimental Aircraft Association's* Reserve Grand Champion Warbird at Oshkosh 1992.

I shall begin with two quotes from a book for which I have the highest regard, the Holy Bible. "A man's wisdom gives him patience." Proverbs 19:11; "The end of a matter is better than its beginning, and patience better than pride." Ecclesiastes 7:8 I credit my God and Lord for giving me the wisdom, patience, and skill to complete this project, THE PURSUIT OF PERFECTION. While it was my task to supervise and co-ordinate the project, it was far from a one man effort. These skilled craftsmen worked long and hard to complete the project, Dan Dilley, Roger Furnish, Gary Koepke, and David Sotka. All of our work was performed under the careful eye of John Dilley. His attention to detail crowned our efforts with success.

Where do you begin a project of this magnitude? For me, the answer was easy. The drip pan under the assembled airplane contained the fluid that would not only start the project but would become the hardest puzzle and most baffling mystery. The leaking Jet Fuel mandated that we start with the fuel system

Top: *The Sabre in August 1989 before it was transported, by road, to Fort Wayne Air Service, Baer Field, Indiana (Ian Roach).* **Left:** *N4689H sits proudly outside at Addison, Texas, its new home with the Cavanaugh Flight Museum.* **Below:** *Work began on solving the fuel leak - Fort Wayne, February 1992 (Dick Phillips). Ex RCAF 23293, the Sabre flew with Targetair and Flight Systems before passing to Southern California Aviation. It had two more owners before being purchased by John Dilley. FWAS were also responsible for a major refurbishment of F-86A G-SABR before it was imported to the U.K.*

TION, it would be majoring in Mediocrity. We would not settle for a seeping Sabre.

Disassemble the aircraft again. Remove the tanks. Test them. Send them out for testing. Out of ideas, we sent one of the tanks back to the manufacturer for testing. Their reply, "The tank doesn't leak." many phone conversations with the tank builder and others would not solve the mystery of leaking fuel; especially one so slow as to take weeks to appear.

Puzzle complete, mystery solved, and a new word added to my vocabulary. During another exasperating conversation with the tank builder, he said, "that wicking could be the problem." "What's wicking?", I asked. He told me that the fibres of the tank have the capacity to act like a wick in an oil lamp whenever they come into contact with fuel. Any opening in the tank, and there are many, would provide an opportunity for fuel to enter the fibres and finally penetrate the outer bladder and a leak

We would end up with a dry airplane and a new word added to my vocabulary that I shall never forget. However, what began in April 1991 would find a new calendar hanging on the wall before we conquered the fuel system.

Fuel was leaking from the aircraft where the centre wing and outer wing panels bolt together. At first, we tried to stop the leak without removing the wings, a labour intensive job (we would get quicker at this.) All efforts failed as the clear fluid persisted in seeping from the wings. Finally, we removed the wings. We would remove and reinstall them *three times* before the stubborn seepage stopped. We would remove all the rubber bladder tanks from the aircraft, test them again and again in our efforts. We would reinstall them and the wings with new gaskets and great care only to have them leak again. Twice the airplane sat with a full load of fuel for over three weeks before a single drop would appear. At this point, some might have been content to, "Let it drip." But this would not be the PURSUIT OF PERFEC-

is born, and a slow leak to boot. But once it's there, it runs like a siphon. Was this our problem and is there a cure? I can now say "yes" to both questions.

The builder told me that they now seal the cross section of any tank opening with a special sealer that provides a fuel barrier. We ordered the expensive sealer, a few ounces makes my wife's costly perfume seem cheap, applied it to every bolt and hole and opening. It worked! After months of bathing daily in jet fuel, enough to fly the Sabre around the world, we finally had a dry airplane! Patience, perseverance, and perspiration, sealed the Sabre!

Of course, we worked on other parts of the aircraft while we pursued the fuel system leak. But it wasn't until the wings were on for good that we could complete other systems. But we tackled it system by system. Puzzle by puzzle,

mystery by mystery, we conquered them all: A leaky hydraulic system would require many new lines and 'O' rings before all three systems were in working order. Once rigged, the landing gear system would perform flawlessly, with the exception of a sticking indicator. Rigging of the flight control systems would also be labour intensive, three weeks on the leading edge slats alone, with a like amount spent on rigging tail controls. The environmental control system contained many puzzles; but gradually our search for missing pieces completed this puzzle. At this point I might add that we had a warehouse full of parts in boxes but no inventory. It was common to spend two to three hours searching for an elusive part. We often left the warehouse with mixed feelings of exhilaration and exasperation; joy when we found a part to complete a system and irrita-

tion when we knew the part was there but we just couldn't find it. Through it all, we plodded forward and completed more systems. The drop tanks would take two men over a month to restore; but they are dent free and they don't leak! Canopy preparation would take one man a month; and yet, with the aircraft in the paint shop and the EAA annual convention at Oshkosh looming on the horizon, we would find ourselves preparing another canopy to take its place.

All the while, we had been working on the electrical system in which we still find much humour, for John Dilley had been told that the aircraft had been *completely rewired*. We found a great deal of slippage in use of the word *completely*. Not counting avionics, we put over 3000 feet of new wire in the cockpit alone. The engine temperature indicator wire would be

the only original wire reinstalled in the harness. Much of the wiring that had been replaced we found ourselves replacing again in our *pursuit of perfection*.

Speaking of perfection causes me to reflect on two more areas - the engine installation and the cockpit. The engine installation had to be perfect. We must get it right the first time. We did not want to have to move it in and out like a yo-yo. This required meticulous checks be carried out on the engine and engine bay prior to installation. We did encounter an oil leak after a test flight but that was easily corrected through engine access panels. By the grace of God the engine went in right the first time and performed stupendously.

The exterior of the aircraft is, beyond doubt, immaculate. Yet the cockpit is indeed the showplace of the airplane. Here the credit by

and large goes to Dan Dilley. Dan restored the ejection seat, built and installed the instrument panel. It is, in every sense, perfect. Pictures do not capture the excellence of his work. Pictures, on the other hand, do show what we had when we started the project - the puzzle - the mystery.

And that brings me back to where I began. I could go on to describe the challenges we encountered in taking the aircraft from the condition it arrived in to the condition it came to be in when it soared again; but a blow-by-blow account would hardly interest anyone. It is the end product that really captures one's attention; and here, more words will not do justice to what the eye will behold. In addition, more words would only seem like boasting on my part. That is not my intention. I would hope that all readers would have the opportunity to

see the picturesque sight of this Sabre's silhouette soaring through God's sky. For He is the one who deserves the real credit in our PURSUIT of PERFECTION. He is the one who gives us the talents, abilities, skills, and most of all the patience to make this an award winning Sabre. It soars to His glory. "The end of a matter is better than its beginning....." Respectfully submitted by Bob Becker of *Fort Wayne Air Service* to the praise, honour and glory of my Lord and Saviour Jesus Christ.

The Editor would like to say a very special thank you to John Dilley at *Fort Wayne Air Service*, and indeed to Bob Becker who answered a 'Mayday' call from me at short notice. Our thanks also to Jim Cavanaugh at *The Cavanaugh Flight Museum* for supplying the excellent photographs of the aircraft today.

Airworthy & Project Sabres

It was felt that this listing was vital, as our main aim is to in this series is to write about Warbirds Today. As you will see from our worldwide Sabre Survey starting on page 67 there is no shortage of airframes for restoration. The airframes listed here are either airworthy (the two F-86Fs still flying with the FAB in Bolivia and recorded recently by Gerry Manning are not listed here - FAB656 and 658)in civilian hands and being operated as warbirds or in a supporting military contract type role.

The airframes listed below all have an interesting history. Should you be interested in this then we strongly recommend that you refer to the latest edition of the Warbirds Worldwide Directory in which John Chapman and Geoff Goodall listed all the surviving Sabres and their histories.

Right: One of the ex RAAF Sabres acquired by Sanders Aviation at Chino in 1989. Another of the aircraft was outside at the time (Paul Coggan)

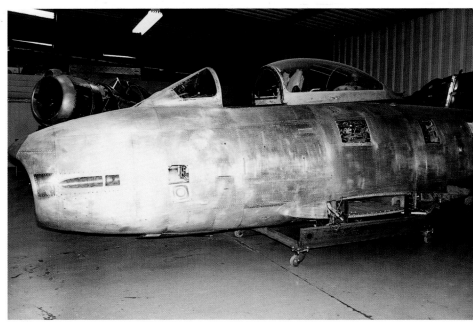

Construction Number	Model	Customer s/n	Registration	Current Owner	Dates
151-	F-86A	48-0178	G-SABR	Golden Apple Operations Ltd, Stamford (shipped to UK, assembled Bournemouth flies as USAF "8178/FU-178")	10.91/92 3.92,
161-318	F-86A	49-1324	N57964	Ben W. Hall, Seattle WA	78/92
172-167	F-86F	51-2884	N57966	Ben W. Hall, Seattle WA	78/92
173-215	F-86D F-86L	51-6071	N86RJ	Robert A. Kemp, Reno NV	3.83/92
176-348	F-86F	51-13417	N51RS	(to Ejercito del Aire as C5-....): del. ex USAFE Mid Atlantic Air Museum, Middletown PA (rest. to fly)	.58 11.87/92
191-304	F-86F	52-4608	N57963	(test bed for Rocketdyne AR2-3 motor) Robert D. Scott, San Martin CA	78/92
191-655	F-86F	52-4959	N105BH	World Wide Aircraft, Miami FL (flies in camouflage scheme)	9.90/92
191-658	F-86F	52-4962	N7006G	(to FA Argentina as C-111) Rick E. Sharpe/Warbirds Unlimited, Rosharon TX	8.88
191-682	F-86F	52-4986	N188RL	Coleman Warbird Museum, Coleman TX D K Precision Inc, Fort Lauderdale FL	6.90/92
191-708	F-86F	52-5012	N4TF	Rick E. Sharpe/Warbirds Unlimited, Rosharon TX Cinema Air, Carlsbad CA	4.90/92
191-812	F-86F	52-5116	N3145T	(to FA Argentina as C-119) Coleman Warbird Museum, Coleman TX	1.92
191-835	F-86F	52-5139	N86F	(to FA Peruana as FAP.......) Tom Wood/Heritage Aircraft Sales, Indianapolis IN (flies as USAF "12849/FU-849")	2.89/92
191-839	F-86F	52-5143	N25143	William Simone, Fountain Valley CA Lesley L. Crowder, Sunland CA	78 84/92

01-484	F-86D	53-1040	N74062	AMCEP Inc, Tucson AZ	87/93
-52	F-86H	53-1250	N31250	Spirit Fighters Inc, Chesterfield MO	5.91/92
44-83	FJ-4B Fury	Bu143575	N9255 N400FS	Flight Systems Inc, Long Beach CA Flight Systems Inc, Mojave CA Larry Mockford, Mojave, CA	.71/78 .78/90 .93
86	Mk. 5 QF-86E	RCAF23096	N74180 (2	Flight Systems Inc, Mojave CA: del. sale rep.	26.7.74/80 86/92
85	Mk. 5	RCAF23195	N5591N	Flight Systems Inc, Mojave CA sale rep., Orlando FL	2.80/86 87/92
012	Mk. 5	RCAF23222	N46882	Flight Systems Inc, Mojave CA sale rep.	2.84 86/92
021	Mk. 5	RCAF23231	N91FS	Tracor Flight Systems Inc, Mojave CA	6.82/92
049	Mk. 5 QF-86E	RCAF23259		Maritime Aircraft Repair & Overhaul/ US Army, Redstone Arsenal AL : USCR	88/92
075	Mk. 5	RCAF23285	N87FS (1 N92FS	Flight Systems Inc, Mojave CA Tracor Flight Systems Inc, Mojave CA	82 6.82/92
083	Mk. 5	RCAF23293	N4689H	Cavanaugh Flight Museum, Addison, Texas	9.93
104	Mk. 5	RCAF23314	N8687D	Combat Jets Flying Museum EAA Aviation Foundation, Oshkosh WI (flies as USAF "12897/The Huff/FU-897")	.92
113	Mk. 5	RCAF23323		US Army, Redstone Arsenal AL : USCR	88/92
120	Mk. 5	RCAF23330	N86JR	Maritime Aircraft Repair & Overhaul/ Combat Jets Flying Museum, EAA Aviation Foundation, Oshkosh WI	.92

bove: This ex Argentine Air Force F-86F is seen here at Chino, California, registered N30CW in 1989. It is now owned by the Coleman arbird Museum in Texas where it is registered N3145T. U.S. serial is 52-5116; it served with the FA Argentina as C-119. (Paul Coggan)

1137	Mk. 5	RCAF23347	N93FS	Tracor Flight Systems, Mojave CA	89
1157	Mk. 5	RCAF23367	N86FS	US Army, Redstone Arsenal AL : USCR	88/92
1294	Mk. 6	RCAF23504	N30CJ	Corporate Jets Inc, Scottsdale AZ (based Deccimomanu, Sardinia : mil. contract .89) (based Soesterberg, Netherlands: mil. contract .91)	4.88/92
1459	Mk. 6	RCAF23669		(to SAAF as 350)	
			N3841V	Flight Systems Inc, Mojave CA	3.83/92
1461	Mk. 6	RCAF23671		(to SAAF as 352)	
			N38301	Corporate Jets Inc, Scottsdale AZ	7.91/92
1468	Mk. 6	RCAF23678		(to SAAF as 359)	
			N3831B	M. D. Aire Co, Encino CA	93
1472	Mk. 6	RCAF23682		(to SAAF as 363)	
			N3842H	Corporate Jets Inc, Scottsdale AZ	92
1474	Mk. 6	RCAF23688		(to SAAF as 365)	
			N106JB	John MacGuire, Fort Hancock TX	4.83
				John MacGuire/War Eagles Air Museum, Santa Teresa NM (flies as SAAF "365")	88/92
1480	Mk. 6	RCAF23690		(to SAAF as 371)	
			N3842J	National Airshows Inc, New Bern NC	8.91/92
1482	Mk. 6	RCAF23692		(to SAAF as 373)	
			N3844E	Darryl G. Greenamyer, Ocala FL	92
1489	Mk. 6	RCAF23699		(to SAAF as 380)	
			N3846J	(noted stored unconv., Mojave 90)	
				Tracor Flight Systems, Austin TX	92
1490	Mk. 6	RCAF23700		(to SAAF as 381)	
				to SAAF Museum	
			N50CJ	Corporate Jets Inc, Scottsdale AZ	12.87/92
				based Soesterberg, Netherlands: mil. contract	91
1491	Mk. 6	RCAF23701		(to SAAF as 382)	
			N87FS (2	Tracor Flight Systems Inc, Mojave CA	4.84/92
1600	Mk. 6	S6-1600		(to Luftwaffe as BB+170)	
		D-9538	N82FS	Flight Systems Inc, Mojave CA	10.81/92
1675	Mk. 6	S6-1675		(to Luftwaffe as BB+284; KE+104)	
			N80FS	Tracor Flight Systems Inc, Mojave CA	10.81/92
1710	Mk. 6	S6-1710		(to Luftwaffe as JB+240)	
		D-9541	N89FS	Flight Systems Inc, Mojave CA	5.81/92
CA27-9	Mk.30	A94-909		RAAF Wagga NSW : inst. airframe	86
				RAAF Richmond NSW: spares for A94-983	88
				Lang Kidby/Transcorp, Redcliffe QLD : dism.	88/89
				Sanders Aviation, Chino CA	89/91
				(rest. to fly, Chino CA)	
CA27-14	Mk.30	A94-914		Sanders Aviation, Chino CA	.89/91
CA27-16	Mk.30	A94-916		Charles Osborne, Louisville, kentucky, Indiana	.93
CA27-70	Mk.32	A94-970		(to TNI-AU/Indonesian AF as inst. airframe)	
				RAAF Richmond NSW : rest. to fly	.88/91
CA27-83	Mk. 32	A94-983		(to R. Malaysian AF as FM1983)	11.71
			VH-PCM	RAAF Historical Flight (flies as RAAF "A94-983")	2.5.88/92
CA27-94	Mk.32	A94-354		(to R. Malaysian AF as FM1354)	10.69
				Sanders Aviation, Chino CA	.89/91
			91	offered at auction, Santa Monica CA: not sold	10.91
CA27-109	Mk.32	A94-369		(to R. Malaysian AF as FM1369)	8.69
				Jeff Trappett, Morwell VIC (rest. to fly)	82/91

Old Hog May Root Again

Ed Buerckholtz of Spirit Fighters Inc. tells the story so far of the acquisition and rebuild to flying condition of a rare North American F-86H

The airport at Rockford, Illinois is a breezy place at almost any time, but as I skated down the slippery southern taxiway in a wailing FH-227 at midnight it looked like a corner of Siberia rejected for lack of interest. I noted a familiar shape softened by snow and gloom away on the east side, and muttered to myself "Geez, a Sabre! I wonder what kind of idiot owns that?" That was in the mid 1970's and little did I imagine that one day I would be the 'idiot' involved in a venture aimed at bringing that very machine back to flight status.

The whole thing began when Leroy Keener, a friend, pilot, mechanic and world traveller saw the plane in 1989 and returned home to say "I saw a pretty good looking Sabre at RFD; let's check it out. It belongs to a Tech school." I recalled the snowy lump I'd seen years before. "I've seen that thing, Lee" I replied, "but forget it. You can't get anything out of a school like that. It's impossible".

"You may say that," rejoined Lee, "and it may be, but you don't really know unless you try!" And so *Spirit Fighters* began.

We went to see the airplane, and Professor Jim Froemming was kind to us. They gave us a copy of the info pack they had prepared for the half dozen fool who came in every year looking for Sabre stuff. It contained a 1987/Winter issue of *Warbirds International* in which appeared a letter from Jim describing the aircraft. Discouragingly prominent in the article was the plain statement: "It cannot be certified for flight." Jim was sympathetic; "Too bad; we really don't use it much any more. The FAA is urging us to get something more mod-

ern." "Oh yeah?" I responded, "what would you like to have?" Jim thought about that. "A nice King Air would suit our needs - PT-6s - yes indeed." We recovered well. We thanked Jim, got on our horses and left.

Thus began a fascinating story. When I got home I told my story to friends. Most simply

said "I could have told you that. What a waste! But one friend, Bob Morgenthaler, had been very successful in aviation, and he said "Sometimes you have to motivate people know what I mean? Let's form a company and buy a King Air." That scared me, but along with Butch Giesman, another successful aviation entrepreneur, we actually did it. Not long after we were no closer to a Sabre, but we were look

***Top:** Sister ship to F-86H 53-1250, which i the subject of this article. Seen here is 53-125 which was displayed at Fort Lauderdale fo many years but is now on a pole in the town Photographed here in 1980 (MAP Photo, **Below:** 'Horse Collar' of Old Hog is polishe since paint retention is doubtful. The radom will be refinished black (Spirit Fighters).*

g at a King Air 90 on the ramp. It lightened ur hip pockets if not our hearts.

Things began to happen in late 1990. We went ▫ RFD and brought some college officials own to St. Louis for lunch. On the ramp we estured casually over our shoulders. "There's ur plane." They looked at it, then us. "We ought it for you. We want to trade." They oked at the plane, closer up this time, since eir feet were walking that way.

It took another year, but the deal was done. involved government agencies we'd never ealt with, documents we'd never heard of, ongress people, administrators, and lawyers aunting in their numbers and their require- ents, but it was done. It's a story in itself, and e I may tell someday. But one day in March 991, a trailer from Ben Nattress's *Worldwide ircraft Recovery* arrived at our home field, the pirit of St. Louis Airport. A new phase of the attle had begun.

The story of 250's rescue is a true chronicle pure luck. We were fortunate enough to find aircraft that had gone to a school where eople respect airplanes, rather than to a play- ound, park, or gate-guard site where thieves arry off whatever vandals do not destroy. We ere blessed in that the school was in a cold imate, where humidity was moderate, and lt air did not exist. We were serendipitous to rive at a time when the school wanted to odate their training inventory. But the loud- st clang of the golden horseshoe was heard hen we learned of the peculiar situation garding the aircraft's supporting paperwork! seemed that the local city government had quested ' an aircraft' to adorn a public park, yet unconstructed, and turned in their quest to the U.S. government. The matter as then forgotten for several years, the city overnment was changed, and the 'park' site eveloped for another purpose. One day the nsuspecting denizens of city hall were star- ed to get a call from the airport dministration: "Your plane is here!" A minion the mayor was dispatched to the field and ere shown the "monster" F-86 HOG still immering with heat from its final flight. here'll be a team in next week to disarm it." as the pilot's comment as he departed to atch his return flight. The airport manager lowed us how he would be happy to know a ate certain on which this nuisance attraction ould be removed from his ramp, and city hall ced an embarrassing situation.

Enter the aviation faculty of Rock Valley ollege (RVC). They agreed to take the orphan , and by way of documentation were given a opy of a copy of a receipt for one (1) F-86H-) (NA-203) condition unspecified. By the time pirit Fighters entered the picture in 1990, this as the only document remaining. Not trans- r, no restriction schedule, no list of onditions, no nothing at all. The normal solu- on in such a case is for the college to ask the SA for a copy of their documents, and the ollege, wanting their King Air waiting on our mp, was happy enough to try. This line of

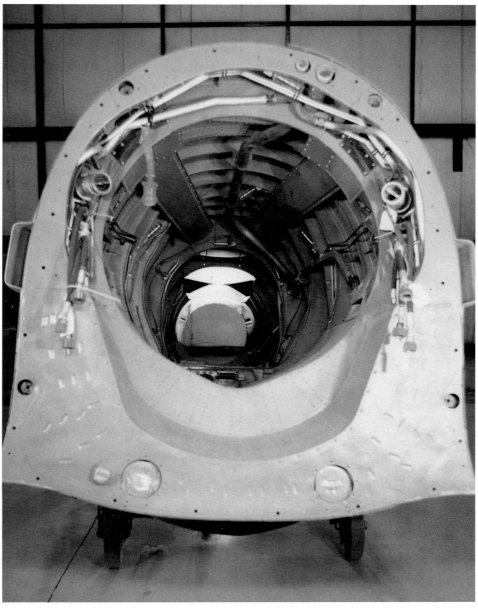

approach fell flat when the GSA revealed that no copy was available. (This was due either to a records fire or to the Paperwork reduction act I forget). In any case, *no dockee, no laundlee*; that was that! As it ultimately turned out, it would have been "that" if they had found the documents, because in 1970 such aircraft were considered weapons systems and restricted from ever leaving government control. By 1990, the aircraft was recognised as what it is now - a demilitarised antique - and release, it seemed, might be obtained. But not if the 1970 document could still have been referred to; it would have governed as if written in stone. The college was able to advance the position that a document is not paper only, it is a concept allowing the creation of a new piece of paper. Predictably, the GSA was not enthusiastic about this idea, but the college caused repre- sentations to be made by certain nameless but highly placed officials, and in time a "new" doc- ument was issued. Hooray! Now we could start the process of petitioning for release of the air- craft to the college. This requires that the property be first offered to all other govern-

Above: The aft fuselage section of the H model is now complete including new flex lines, some new hard lines to replace chafed ones and a complete clean up and reprime after repairs where necessary (Spirit Fighters)

ment agencies, entities, and bureaus, then to other eligible donees, etc., and then finally, in the absence of any takers, a release is obtained. This understandably takes some months, but in the end it was done. The col- lege now owned the airplane.

One might think that were home free, but foolish indeed would be the simple soul who so believed, for faculties have administrations, and administrations have lawyers! It was time for another nail from the golden horseshoe, and we got it: the head lawyer was an old B-17 pilot, and friendly to the cause. With his kind assistance we made the bills of sale, hold harmless agreements, memoranda of under- standing etc., and closed the deal, laying out all the copies of all the papers on two cafete- ria tables for the signature of all the worthies involved. It was a snowy day, but clear above, and the old King Air made its last flight with

Above: the tail end of the F-86H. Hot section skin will be polished and the aircraft will be painted metallic light gray overall. (Spirit Fighters)

panache, taxying in to the waiting arms of the faculty. Now there is one old bird that has a good home. We hoped that we would provide one just as good for our *Sabre Hog*. Note the *our*.

"Puttin' it on here boss!" February in Rockford is cold and blustery, and our mechanic, Pat Fenwick, was struggling in an unheated hangar to loosen dozens of wing bolts whose 16 point heads had long been immersed in icy water-filled cavities on the upper surface of the wing roots. In about half the cases, the rusty heads would round off immediately, rendering further efforts with a wrench useless. Pat and Leroy had rigged up a flex-drive power head with a mean-looking cutting burr; it looked like a dental drill for a whale. With this formidable instrument, they removed the heads without damaging the wing structure, and the wings were pulled off. A support frame for the fuselage was welded up, and the whole plane was set on a 'low-boy' trailer with the help of *Worldwide Aircraft Recovery*, Inc., fresh from the challenging delivery of deactivated SR-71s all over the country. These guys are good. The

plane arrived at our field (SUS) one rainy March day, the driver regaling us with the hazards of transporting 'interesting' loads on a public highway. It seems everybody starts gawking and quits steering, with the result that the mission is under attack the whole way. With the F-86H safely off-loaded in our hangar, dry and warm, we executed, one after another the boldface items of a four point check list: 1. Apply 28V External power. 2. Raise canopy (it works!) 3. Climb into cockpit. 4. Elevate Champagne glass and drink!

When you are recruiting technicians for a jet warbird rebuild, the guy who answers the ad often turns out to be (a) very excited but inexperienced,(b) 'experienced' but not entirely truthful, or (c) the kind of guy who has worked on everything all over the world, but is currently installing seamless guttering from the back of a truck, selling real estate, and (in season) preparing tax returns. So when you do find a real artist, you tend to overlook a few peculiarities.

I tell you this so you will understand that when I found two of our 'techs sitting on a tug laughing hysterically at ten in the morning, I was looking for the beer cans. The truth was worse, and we came close that day to providing the raw material for containers to hold 'a thousand

pints of lite.' It seems that while hoisting our J-73G-E off its temporary resting place on aircraft jacks, the main support cable holding the boom erect had parted. Fortunately the engine was only an inch in the air, and descended firmly back from whence it came. Another inch and we might have been ringing up the scrap dealer while we wondered what to tell the banker. Just a regular day in the restoration business!

I have long been accustomed to talking to warbird restorers in *Lots Land* (Zip 91710), and when they face a problem it's "no problem, we'll just bring it up from billet." Soon we go to this unenviable pass ourselves. It appears that when North American Aviation wanted to seal the gap between the retracted flap and the top of the wings, they assigned the task to an engineer I would truly like to meet, though not in any dark corners. This worthy decided the situation required a complex extrusion of fine magnesium, unnecessary though this might seem to we who know less. This precious object was then milled to fit by a machinist of the same balmy stripe, and installed with 344 rivets in a way requiring disassembly of the rear wing structure to get it off. In due time, these seals corroded away, as magnesium will, and by the time the Sabre came to us they were good only as blades for the world's longest cheese-cutter. We were lucky. It required a search of only two months to find John Patton, a machinist who could and would mill replacements, this time out of a hard grade of aluminium. We even have an extra set, so I now have a valuable bargaining chip when bargaining with recalcitrant lotus-landers who are hankering to begin an F-86H restoration of their very own!

Another amusing feature of the restoration experience is the Easter-egg hunt for parts. We were truly fortunate in that Jim Froeming and the guys at the college protected the aeroplane from vandals and souvenir hunters, but the government had demilitarised the bird in 1970 and the team that did it must have had one hot collective date, because they removed not only everything dangerous or classified, but they did it in the manner requiring the fewest twists of the wrist, taking the chaff with the wheat. As a result, we are currently searching for things that were in no way hazardous or secret. Trying to replace them allows one the opportunity of meeting several interesting types of characters. One is what I call the 'pack-rat'. This is the guy that has it, but will not sell it, even though he has no use for it now or in the foreseeable future. This fellow has no rational justification for his position and needs none. He has the goods. Price escalation is generally useless; the method of choice is barter. A B-25 turret drive for a new canopy. Voila! Friends for life.

Another distinctive character is the 'big dealer' His position is that he has no time to do such a small transaction. A canopy seal. It would take more time to find it than it's worth. Usually these guys are equipped with computer inventory systems. I believe that the true reason for their reluctance is that they are hoping to sell all their stuff to our government (or some other government) at gold plated prices. Needless to say, antiquarian sentiment is not part of their makeup. The answer is an intermediary - a mutual friend who can put the request on a more personal basis. 'Rainmakers' like this have helped many a desperate restorer. May their tribe increase!

A third thorn in the restorers side is what I call the 'ice-cream syndrome', in honour (?) of the Sacramento overrun accident which could have done away with the jet movement once and for all. This mind-set can be found anywhere. It even pervades the halls of the original manufacturers, especially if they have been through a merger or three. Their position is that any assistance, let alone sale of physical objects, to restorer opens the door, however slightly, to a disastrous legal judgement. After talking to one of these guys, I am always left with a mental picture of a small, haggard wretch in deep mourning, entombed in a basement office with a cloud over his head, while in the distance the voice of doom can be heard intoning the dread phrase: "jointly and severely liable". There's not a whole lot one can do about the ice-cream parlour syndrome. It would help if the safety record of the jet warbird movement would improve just a bit. The military can get away with wrecking jets; it usually occurs in deserts, at sea, or at military airfields in grubby spots far from public observation. Further, it is necessary for the common defence. But when civilians do it, it is often at public displays. Sometimes they even take journalists in to the smoking hole with them. Better they should take a lawyer, but be that as it may, nobody will forget Sacramento.

The work on our F-86H is progressing nicely. The aft section is done, and looks like new, thanks to Leroy Keener. The wings will be done as will the wheels and brakes, by the time this is published. Would you believe 256 new brake pucks? The forward bays of the fuselage are done as are the tail feathers.

Still waiting are the cockpit and the main hydraulics bay, the main gear wells, and the engine inspection. With only 180 hours on it, the J-73 looks pretty good. We have a guy to plan the avionics set-up, and we are prepared to bite the bullet and make it a good one, with modern gyros, possibly EFIS, GPS nav, and all the necessary. Can anybody get a line on a HUD projector?

Another thing readers might help us with is the weapons bay display we want to fix up on the right side. We want to be able to remove the gun bay panel and have everything there. The bay is already redone, but we need the M-39 cannons and the adapt kit and ammo feed drives. Needless to say the weapons will be inoperable, but we want them to look good. Present plans call for a conformal smoke-oil tank in the left gun bay. Baggage space might be found in the ammo lockers, or maybe in external stores. Does anybody have a Mk.12

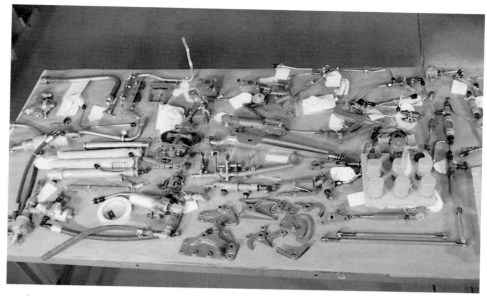

Above: To give you some idea of the complexity of the restoration and the lengths Spirit Fighters are going to ensure the quality of restoration this photograph shows the components from the nose gear well awaiting re-installation. (Spirit Fighters Inc.)

nuclear device training shape? Golf clubs would be better than megadeaths - titanium instead of plutonium!

Once again we appeal to the kindness of strangers; send us your tired, your poor F-86H stuff. We still don't have a canopy seal, but we do have six extra F-86H nose wheel tyres. We're hunting for initiators and catapults for canopy and seat, but we have lots of corporate jet parts, Sabreliner, Falcon and the like. We even have a pair of F-86H flap-gap seals - new manufacture! For you, a special deal.

We're always on the line here, and interested in talking to Sabre folks. Call (314)532-2707 of Fax (314)532-1486

In the days of the great sailing vessels, the period immediately after departure was a busy one - getting store in order, shaking down an unhandy grew, securing and repairing all the inevitably carries away in the first hard blow - these things kept everyone occupied and more. Likewise, the approach to harbour was an exciting time, with many preparation to make and new experiences awaiting ashore. The long weeks or even months between, the middle passage were nevertheless the time which most formed and tested the truly nautical cast of mind. Further, the most seasoned salt could be brought near to tears of frustration by the intrusion of days or weeks of calm - 'in the doldrums' - with the ship wallowing without way in an ever widening collection of flotsam, jetsam and filth.

So it was with our restoration of 53-1250 in October '92. We had begun well; the aft section and both wings were complete, all actuators overhauled, all damage and corrosion repaired. The canopy (a complete assembly, as it has to be operable electrically, manually and pyrotechnically, and carries the cabin pressure control systems well) is well on the road to better than new under the hand of Larry Denning, a builder whose aircraft won Grand Champion at Oshkosh. A good start has been made on the fuselage, with gun and forward bays complete, but like the old mariners we were 'becalmed' by the loss of our central

mechanic, and the search for a replacement, even in this time of aerospace unemployment, has produced a motley and rag-tag assortment of 'specialists' who are accustomed to doing only a rigidly defined sub-part of a task. What we needed was a restorer, an artist!

Like the old sailor scratching a backstay or (softly) trying to "whistle up a wind", we plotted and schemed, trying to snare the right true restorer whose tribe apparently has decreased. Rumour and travellers' tales reached us of a far land in which real F-86H's bellowed no more than ten years ago, well IRAN'd, fitted with remote flight equipment and redesignated QF-86H, all (alas) now gone to Davy Jones' locker. But the men who maintained and modified then are some of them still there living quietly in their high desert home near Tom Wolfe's 'rat-shack plains of Olympus.'

Now let it be clear that these mad-monk mechanics reside in Lotus Land whose secret name is California! If you are a novice in these matters, let me advise you: outside his area code (much less the Midwest, and still less (ugh) Missouri) the result is predictable: deafness, doctors' orders to remain in a warm dry climate, children need day care, wife terminally ill, a man's bowels upset by the very suggestion. So unless these objections can be overcome by lucrative offers, or unless we can somehow revive the press-gang tactics of Portsmouth, we are at a stand.

This difficulty had reached the point where radical solutions had to be considered. One was raising the ante to the point where our man couldn't afford *not* to come. This is expensive. Another was moving our project, bag and baggage, and bandsaw, to the rat-shack plains. That was expensive too, but we had to consider it. At least there is a potential ally in Dan Sabovich, the manager of Mojave airport, and one of the few such officers who considers it his duty to further his clients' projects rather than frustrating them. Again, there are long runways, test ranges near at hand, an FAA office with experience in this sort of thing, and, if matters in flight testing deteriorate to the point of maybe or maybe not, there is the big white friendly lake bed not faraway. Hmmm, maybe not a bad idea. We have to do something, that' for sure.

The middle passage; when will it end? one day the end will be in sight, and, in the grip of 'channel fever' , we will (literally) be contracting for the services of the pilot. The day seems far away.

April is icumen in
Loud cry "restore"
Outsweep gray winter's dust.
Open - O hangar door!

While media attention predictably focused on snows in the Boston-Washington strip, and Floridians got blown away, it went nearly unnoticed that March, 1993 saw St. Louis buried under not one but two unseasonable blizzards. Followed by two air masses that the forecasters cheerily call 'continental polar'. Higher gas bills and less work done as a result, apparently justifying in part the 'lotus-landers' scornful query: can any good thing come out of the Midwest? Our answer: Maybe, if we can find some good mechanics.

Actually, we seem on the verge of a breakthrough, though it may be unwise to suggest it. We, of course, are not superstitious, but like Napoleon we believe in the incompleteness of information and the reality of luck. We have

one very craftsmanlike young man who appeared on our hangar apron after having finished a CASA Saeta using only crudely translated Spanish manuals originally written with a truly peninsular disdain for detail. We inspected and found quite a creditable job. His work in the very cruddy nosegear itself is a work of art that we display in the general offices. Now this week we are looking at two additional fellows with F-86 backgrounds who are being laid off by a certain St. Louis-based aerospace company whose federal largesse has been somewhat squeezed of late. If we can do deal with them, we may begin in April with cautious optimism.

Our wings are done. Our aft section is done. Our landing gear systems are almost done. We have a guy to start inspecting the J-73. (Casual inspection shows a most disturbing array of cracks in the after case. Weldable, (according to the book !) We sure could use a J-73 illustrated parts bulletin (J-73-GE-3) but can't find one. The ejection seat hardware continues to be a thorn in our side. All the instruments have to be checked and/or overhauled, and we have no manuals for that. Terror grips us as we face the task of designing a whole new avionics package capable of coping with the modern airspace, as hostile in its demands as the one the *Old Hog* was designed to penetrate, in some ways. We want it to look and act military, but modern and user friendly. Our limited panel space cries out for a heads up display. We'll never have a true HOTAS (hands on throttle and stick, stupid) capability, but there are a few

extra grip switches that could do something else, since we aren't going to shoot 20mm any more. Then there is also the M-39 cannon question; we'd like to have the right side open up onto a first class display, with belts and ammo and all. And what about the old Mark 12 nuclear weapon? Could there be a training shape left somewhere we could trade for? The only one I know of is in the National Atomic Museum at Albuquerque. If we seem to have a lot of questions and no answers, that's because we do! Or so it seems as we spread our lawn fertiliser in the March wind.

A lot of water has flowed down the Rock River in Illinois since 28 May, 1970, when a bottle-cap colonel named Joe Radoci landed 53-1250 for the last time at the town named for a crossing nearby. A few more gallons will escape before the *Old Hog* snorts again, but now we are bold enough for the first time, to assert that it actually will. And on top of everything this 31 March, 1993 in gravy dirty old St.Louis, it is absolutely, undeniably SPRING. **WW Ed Buerckholtz.**

The story of the Old Hog continues to be told in the regular Sabre Jet Classics. We hope to follow the adventures and triumphs of Spirit Fighters in future editions of the Warbirds Worldwide Journal. Our thanks to Ed and to Rick Mitchell of Sabre Jet Classics for allowing us to reprint the story.

Below: An idea of what the finished F-86H will look like is provided by the example at the Pima County Air Museum, Tucson, Arizona (Duncan Curtis)

● 499 Pages ● 134 Piston types ● 42 Jet types detailed

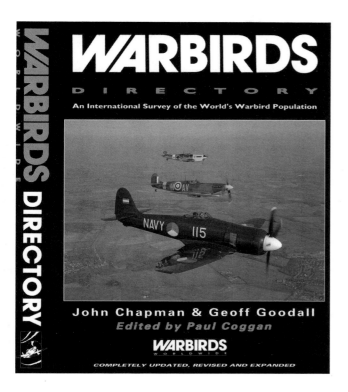

WARBIRDS DIRECTORY

WARBIRDS
D I R E C T O R Y

An International Survey of the World's Warbird Population

NAVY 115

John Chapman & Geoff Goodall
Edited by Paul Coggan
WARBIRDS WORLDWIDE

COMPLETELY UPDATED, REVISED AND EXPANDED

A - You're Adorable

Though it seems like only yesterday, I've just realised that my interest in the Sabre stretches back to late 1974, when I saw pictures of an F-86 being operated in the USA. One look was all it took to ignite a passion for this aircraft. It's somehow ironic that, nearly 19 years later, here I am writing an article about the very aircraft which started it all off - F-86A serial 48-178. I have also been lucky to see this aircraft in the flesh and talk to some of the people who are associated with

Duncan Curtis investigates the history behind the Golden Apple Trust's rare North American F-86A and introduces some of the service people that flew here during service with the military

it, past and present. 48-178 was produced at North American Aviation's Los Angeles factory

as the 50th F-86A dash 5, the first production version for the USAF. '178's constructors number was 43547 and the engine originally fitted was the General Electric J-47GE-7 which developed some 5340lbs thrust. Part of an order for 188 F-86A-5s placed on 20th November 1946 '178 was delivered to the USAF on 18th April 1949 just over a month after the name Sabre was officially adopted.

The aircraft was assigned to the 1st Fighter Group (FG) based at March Air Force base in alifornia. It is thought that the Sabre was then etached to the Strategic Air Command's 9143 terceptor Flight, but by April 1950 the aircraft was with the 94th Fighter Interceptor quadron (IFS) at March AFB. Part of the 1st G the 94th FIS was the first USAF squadron o receive the Sabre. Their Squadron badge as the famous 'Hat in Ring which had originated in World War I. The squadron's main task as defence of the North American factory at os Angles, and their Sabres wore a large scalped green flash along the fuselage sides, with e Hat in Ring badge superimposed on it. ecords show that by 7th April 1950, '178 had een fitted with a 5450lb thrust J-47GE-13 ngine, serial number GE-041467. This engine ad 66:20 hours on it, whilst 178 had logged 10;10 flying hours. Crew Chief for the aircraft : this time was Staff Sergeant Harold K. Shaw. uring the month, the aircraft had experienced roblems with cabin refrigeration and inoperive attitude and slave gyros.

On 15th march 1951, '178 passed to the 56th ghter Interceptor Group, and served with ther the 62nd or 63rd FIS, as the other quadron in the Group, the 61st, was, by then perating the F-94 Starfire. Duty with the group as short however, for on 2nd August 1951, e aircraft was assigned to the 93rd FIS at rtland AFB, New Mexico. Under the control 34 Air Division, 93 FIS were tasked with the efence of the Los Alamos nuclear facility. quadron colours consisted of a red-white-red and around the intake, repeated on the tail

fin above the serial number. The squadron badge, caricatured bird holding a club, was applied to both sides of the fuselage, roughly above the centre of the wing root.

48-178 was modified to F-86A-7 standard at around this time. The main reason for the change in designation was the replacement of the AN/APG-5C radar and Mk 18 gunsight with the AN/APG-30 radar and A-1CM gunsight. This work was carried out under contract AF-18188, probably at Fresno, California.

USAF records then state that '178 went to the 469 FIS at McGhee-Tyson airport, Tennessee in May 1953 and remained there for a year. 469 FIS does not appear on 'official' lists of F-86A squadrons but Bill Van Dine, who was assigned to the squadron in March 1954 recalls: "I cannot confirm that bird ('178) was ever at McGhee-Tyson, but.......I was assigned to the 469th FIS which at the time owned 24 brand new dash 40 F-86Ds and six F-86As."

On 11th may 1954, the Sabre passed from active USAF to the 196th Fighter Bomber Squadron (FBS), California Air National Guard (CA ANG), based at Ontario International Airport. Crew Chief from this time was Ernie Y. Finn, and the aircraft became the personal mount of squadron commander Colonel Arthur H. Bridge. Ernie Finn remembers '178 well: "It was a good flying machine and suffered no mishaps while we had it. I recall that for many months after assignment it had a very unusual high time engine installed, certainly more time than any other engine in the unit. I

remember it became a challenge to see how many hours we could achieve prior to its need for a complete overhaul."

The colour scheme applied to 48-178 consisted of a black bordered yellow tail flash and the script CALIF ANG either side of the fuselage star and bar. It is fairly certain that the markings ANG 178 were carried in large letters above the right hand wing and below the left hand wing. Arthur Bridge became commanding officer of 163 Fighter Group (parent group of 196 FBS) on 12th may 1958, and by this time, '178 was the aircraft assigned to Archie Nogle. Archie had previously flow Sabres with 35FBS in Korea. At around this time, the serial presentation carried on the tail was changed from '8178' to 80178.

During May 1958, 196FBS began to convert to the F-86D Sabre, and '178 was one of the last A models in the squadron. 194FBS, California Air National Guard, based at Fresno who had also flown A-model Sabres then had the idea of obtaining a Sabre for display. Archie Nogle takes up the story: "We had gotten a Telex from Fresno, stating that they wanted this particular number - my number -, '178, and we were talking about it and they said "well,

shoot, who's airplane it that?' and I said "It's mine!", and they said "well, all right, you fly it over to Fresno!". And so I picked out a day, and about 9 or 10 o'clock in the morning I took off, flew by Lompoc (where Archies' wife was treated to an impromptu display) and dropped it off".

There, '178 might have ended her days, but for some reason or other, the Fresno HQ decided to display another F-86A, 49-1272 (which incidentally is still there), and '178 then passed to a vocational school in the area (does anyone know which school or have any photographs of the aircraft at this time? - Editor). Some time later, Glen Wackhold, a Fresno surplus store owner, bought the Sabre at a public auction held by the school. He then towed it back to his storage yard outside Fresno. The 'plane sat in the yard for many years until, in 1970, the aircraft was brought to the attention of Jim Larsen in Seattle, Washington. The prospect of owning a historic jet was too much for Larsen, and he bought '178, unseen, for $700.00. Ben Hall, a well known P-51 and T-6 owner who also lived in Seattle, then became interested in the aircraft and so, in late June 70 they both travelled down to Fresno to see what they had let themselves in for........

The passage of years had left '178 a shadow of her past self. On first inspection, there was found to be a gaping hole where the engine should have been. many panels were missing, and the cockpit had been well gutted. On the plus side there was minimal corrosion to the airframe and luckily the majority of missing panels, plus a very well preserved canopy were found in a nearby warehouse. On this basis, Ben Hall became the proud owner of an F-86A for $1000, a far cry from the $178,000 that North American had billed the USAF in 1949. Fortunately, 48-1278 had not been 'de-milled' at the end of its service career (demobilisation by cutting, among other things, the main spars), and so presented a good prospect for rebuild to flying condition. Hall managed to acquire parts from another F-86A whilst at Fresno and a week after dismantling the aircraft, a lorry load of Sabre parts arrived in Seattle.

Ben Hall then set about the process of putting '178 back into the air. Much time was spent trying to acquire serviceable leading edge slats. Just when it was thought that the problem had been solved, and after much work had been expended in renovating two slat assemblies, disaster struck. It was found that the slat assemblies were not compatible with '178's wing leading edge structure. Due to modifications during production of the early sabres, there were discovered to be many variations in slat assemblies. A quick decision was made to fix the slats in the permanently closed position, and a wing fence was installed, similar to that found on later versions of the F-86. Other missing components were searched for and eventually found and `Hall managed to locate two engines and bought these for $50 each, having previously spent another $1500 for

another engine which turned out to be junk. By the Spring of 1973 the engine was ready to run in the airframe. However, though the engine would start, it would not run properly,

and flamed out when the throttle lever was retarded. Six months of frustration followed trying to trace the fault. It was eventually discovered that the fuel control switch had been

installed upside down in the instrument panel; Hall had been trying to start the engine in the 'emergency' mode.

In the cockpit, many changes were made in the interests of ergonomics. The instruments were placed in a light grey panel, and many of the 'military' items, including the gun sight were not refitted. The ejector seat was also replaced with a fixed item, in the interests of comfort. Though the process of placing '178 on the US Civil register was initiated in September 1970 it took many letters and telephone calls from Ben Hall to finally be allocated the registration N68388, nearly two years later. The registration was applied onto an attractive executive jet style colour scheme which was predominantly white with a red/orange/yellow cheat line.

By January 1974, all the bugs had been ironed out and taxi tests were completed. Paul Bennett, who flew the Boeing Sabre chase plane was selected to carry out the first flight which went almost perfectly on 24th February 1974 from Paine Field, Washington. Ben Hall was later checked out on the aircraft, which made its public debut at Abbotsford later in

the year. Here, the legendary Bob Hoover put on an aerobatic performance in the Sabre. His words say it all - "In all honesty, it is one of the nicest flying airplanes I have had the pleasure of piloting." After this, Ben Hall flew seven or eight shows a year.

At one point, N68388 was fitted with a second seat under its long canopy, becoming the third two seat Sabre to fly. In October 1983, the aircraft was re-registered as N178, and around this time a spurious Korean war-type paint scheme was applied. By this time Hall was finding the Sabre to be an expensive proposition. A half hour routine was costing over $200 in fuel alone. Thus, in 1989, '178 passed to John Dilley at Fort Wayne Air Service in Indiana. Here, Golden Apple Trust, a UK based organisation commissioned FWAS to return the cockpit to its 1949 specification, including the re-installation of an armed ejection seat. The seat which '178 flies with today is a Mitsubishi assembled version as fitted to Japanese F-86Fs. Modern Avionics were also fitted by FWAS prior to test flying by Chuck Scott.

N178 was imported to the UK at the end of 1992. Jet Heritage, as acknowledged experts in jet fighter operations were chosen by Golden Apple to operate and maintain the Sabre. After assembly, '178, now registered as G-SABR took to the air on 21st May 1992 piloted by Adrian Gjertsen. During the 25 minute flight from Hurn airport which was carried out with the undercarriage down, the only problems encountered were with the radios. The UK public debut then followed at the Biggin Hill Air Fair. Other shows were flown during the year and after minor maintenance tasks had been performed during the winter of 1992/93, G-SABR is poised for another busy airshow season.

It's hard to believe that this aircraft is 44 years old - that's older than many of the people who gaze up in wonder at her during an airshow. All I can say is that she looks remarkably well for it. WW Duncan Curtis.

The author would like to thank Earnest Y. Finn and Archie Nogle for their help in the preparation of this feature.

Australia's CAC SABRES

James Kightly outlines the development of the CAC Sabre and reviews activities based around the survivors.

The F-86 Sabre has been said to be one of the most successful fighter aircraft of all time, a view confirmed with hindsight and one reason it was so successful was undoubtedly that it was a finely balanced design, the compromise of firepower, speed and manoeuvrability being near perfect.

Nevertheless, improvements were sought by various agencies; the people at North American Aviation upped the power end of the scales by beefing up the airframe to accept the General Electric J73-GE-3D engine and adding four M39 20mm cannon in the H as against the six .50 calibre guns of the more familiar E and F Sabre variants. However, despite the intention to make this the ultimate North American Sabre, the changes were too late, considering the pace of fighter development at the time, with the additional puff of the new engine not being enough to push the aircraft through the sound barrier in level flight, while the cannon was to give a number of metal fatigue problems. Development would have ironed the latter problem out, but the F-100 Super Sabre was by then on its way.

In Australia it is often held that the Commonwealth Aircraft Corporation Sabre was the best of the breed. Arguments will always rage about the relative merits of type and subtype for any aircraft, and balanced against the fact that the CAC Sabre never served in the same numbers as the North American and Canadair versions or had the same amount of front line usage, it is undeniable that the Australian aircraft retained the superb handling characteristics of the aircraft and increased the effectiveness of the design in two areas that fighter pilots are never satisfied with. The firepower increased and the power was greater.

In the words of Squadron Leader 'Frawls' Frawley; "The F-86 design was modified by CAC to incorporate the Rolls-Royce Avon engine, producing 7,250lbs of thrust (against 5910 of the General Electric J-47-GE-27 engine in the 'F') making it the most powerful Sabre built. It seems that part of the penalty for this increase in thrust was of course fuel consumption, and the aircraft were later modified to remove the leading edge slats and replace them with 'wet' fixed leading edges. I cannot comment on the difference in turn rates because I have not flown a Sabre with leading edge slats. An Avon Sabre can easily be distinguished from other Sabres in that the intake has a three inch high insert or plug in each sidewall to allow for greater intake air as required by the British engine. Australia also removed the six machine

bove: The RAAF static display production ample of the Sabre at RAAF Point Cook in 92. A94-910 looks immaculate, trimmed in d and with all the detailed stencils (James ightly).

uns and replaced them with two 30mm can-ons.

The greater mass airflow was not the only dif-rence that the Avon forced upon CAC esigners by the choice of the Rolls Royce ngine; the lighter, shorter and fatter Avon had be located further aft in the fuselage, caus-g the Aussie version to have a differently onfigured fuselage, breakline and auxiliary takes. The result was an even more crowded ear fuselage, to the extent that the smoke pipe equired by all good aerobatic team aircraft ad to be ducted along the outside like an over-oked piece of plumbing on the many display rcraft the RAAF used. The summary was a selage with only 40% commonality with the orth American F-86F, resulting from 268 engi-eering changes.

It had been chosen for the RAAF against stiff *uy B*ritish opposition effectively by Lawrence ʼackett of CAC alone. With the recommenda-on that the Avon be substituted as the rcraft's engine, by none other than Lord ives of Rolls-Royce, it was hoped that most eople would be happy with the choice. In the vent the modification programme, despite its omplexity, went remarkably smoothly, and .A.C.'s latest aircraft was a hit with the Air orce once again. It is interesting to note that

a serious proposal to buy enough North American Sabres to equip No.77 Squadron, RAAF in Korea, was floated in 1950 but was scotched by a lack of U.S. Dollar finance and the pro-British lobby. The RAAF were stuck with Gloster Meteors instead.

The Avon Sabre did undergo some develop-ment in its time, the effective punch of two 30mm Aden cannon being supplemented in the hard '6-3' wing aircraft with Sidewinder A.A.M.; a most effective weapon for the RAAF. Small export numbers were sold on to the Royal Malaysian Air Force and the Indonesian Air Force later in the aircraft's career, but despite the C.A.C. developed machine's mer-its by the time it was well established in service it was being overtaken by supersonic aircraft.

Avon Sabres Today

Currently there is only one example of the Avon Sabre airworthy in the world, rightfully owned by the RAAF Museum. It is A94-983, registered for convenience as VH-PCM.

Most aircraft are content with one 'first flight', and a number of restored machines with two, but '983 has accomplished no less than three. November 1957 saw the aircraft take to the air for the first time being then one of a large num-ber of C.A.C. Sabres which were putting the RAAF jet pilots back into the front rank of fighter drivers. After a three week period with the Aircraft Research and Development Unit (A.R.D.U.) at Laverton, the Sabre was posted to 78 Fighter Wing, going to RAAF Butterworth in Malaya, where the RAAF were maintaining a major presence during this period, joining No. 3 Squadron there.

Due to a crash-landing on 5th February 1959, the aircraft was returned to Australia where repairs were carried out by C.A.C. at Avalon; the repaired aircraft being then allocated to No. 76 Squadron. After a varied but (from the official records) not over exciting career, the Sabre was sold to the R.M.A.F., under the

Australian Foreign Aid Programme in operation at the time. The Sabre became R.M.A.F. serial number FM1983, allocated to No. 11 Squadron and serving its new owners in a dark green scheme until 1976 when the now very outdated aircraft was grounded to await disposal and scrapping.

That should have been the end, but the RAAF were still maintaining a presence at Butterworth and No. 75 squadron (by then operating Mirage III O) spotted the old warrior and decided to try and give the Sabre a new lease of life. After a great deal of work by the Squadron's engineers, the aircraft took to the air again on July 7th in the hands of Wing Commander 'Mick' Parer. Given this initiative, the aircraft was handed back to the RAAF by the RMAF and was brought back to Richmond, NSW in the hold of a Lockheed C-130. No. 2 Aircraft Depot at Richmond began a full restoration to bring the aircraft back to a more representative operational condition, with (inert) Sidewinders and drop tanks, as well as an external smoke tube along the port rear fuselage. After this work had been completed satisfactorily on March 26th 1981, Squadron Leader David Leach flew the aircraft for its airtest and third 'first flight'!

Its subsequent history has not been without interest, as in 1985 the aircraft suffered a flameout, and was brought in to land by the pilot who chose to attempt to save her rather than obey instructions to punch out which are normal for the type. As narrated elsewhere in this publication, '983 has also attempted to terminally interest Squadron Leader Frawley,

Continued on Page 66

Below: A94-906, Moorabin Aircraft Museum's example of the C.A.C. Sabre looks rather worse for wear at present, but once the planned new hangar is constructed it will be restored to the same excellent standard as the other museum aircraft. (James Kightly)

SPORTS CAR

SHOW TIME!

Flying the RAAF's CAC Sabre

Left: Basking in the Australian sunshine is this Avon powered CA-27 Sabre Mk.31, serial A94-915 of The Marksmen aerobatic team from No. 2 Operational Conversion Unit. The trim is black and yellow. Shown here in 1968 (Adrian Balch collection)

sonally experienced this unpleasant trait while conducting some currency training.

I elected to re familiarise myself with the approach configuration stall characteristics during a mission, and to do this I climbed to 10,000 feet. Because of the aircraft's longitudinal stability, I neglected to look at the skidall prior to entry to the stall. An un-noticed slight imbalance at the point of stall resulted in a minor nose slice to the left which I dutifully decided to arrest with the rudder. The aircraft immediately flipped onto its back whereupon a flurry of activity was needed to prevent over-speeding the undercarriage and flaps, and of course, once that procedure was dealt with, there remained the little matter of a fully developed spin. (which, incidentally, is a prohibited manoeuvre in the Australian Sabre.) The outcome was 7,000 feet lost in altitude and a severely battered ego. The operations manual gives a minimum speed around the base of 150 kts and you can be sure that is strictly adhered to.

The other unpleasant characteristic is the pitch of stability of the Sabre. With the advent of aircraft capable of easily obtaining the transonic region of flight came the need for powered flight controls to allow for the manoeuvrability required of such fighter aircraft. The technology was obviously new and all the problems were not solved in the Sabre, and to cap it all the designers fitted the aircraft with a full flying tailplane as well, resulting in an enormously powerful set of pitch controls. At high (>450 kts) speed a deft touch is required on the controls to prevent the pilot induced oscillations (PIOs).

It is quite easy to exceed the structural limits of the aircraft with only a slight movement of the stick. The RAAF lost a pilot and aircraft in Darwin when, after dispatching a Canberra he decided to pass the hapless bomber and demonstrate the speed and agility of the Sabre with a high speed pull into the vertical. It is not known how much G he achieved, but the wings capped above the aircraft and on inspection during the subsequent enquiry, the imprint of one wingtip was found on the other only two of three inches to the rear of centre, indicating the almost instantaneous structural collapse achieved by the pilot.

All that aside, the aircraft is a delight to fly and in my case to demonstrate. Like any aircraft it has its vices, and as long as you pay particular attention to those areas and avoid them you have no cause for concern.

The Avon Sabre is far superior to the MiG-15 (I am current on both aircraft, and I believe in that regard I am probably the only person who is), it outclimbs, out accelerates and out turns the MiG-15. In a recent exercise to endorse another pilot on the Sabre we used the MiG-

Squadron Leader Frawls' Frawley, RAAF, details the attributes and vices of the Royal Australian Air Force Historic Flight's beautiful CAC Sabre VH-PCM

The Sabre is a delightful aircraft to fly and is a true 'sports car'. Conversion to the aircraft is an interesting (and exciting) experience as only a limited number of dual control Sabres were ever built by North American Aviation, and Australia did not purchase any. That means that the first flight is also the first solo and that encourages adrenaline to flow, believe me.

The Sabre has some nasty habits; the main one being that if you stall the aircraft in the approach configuration whilst turning, the Sabre will flip on to it's back, and if my memory serves me correctly the RAAF lost three aircraft and their pilots in that manner. I per-

Squadron Leader Frawley has his foot on the ammo tray for the Aden cannon, the open access hatch being below the cockpit. VH-PCM, like all service CAC SAbres is very heavily stencilled all over. In fact the aircraft can produce hours of reading! (James Kightly)

15 for formation practice and as the student had flown the Sabre previously, we briefed a l v l air combat tactics exercise as part of the mission, with me in the MiG and the student in the Sabre. The only proviso was that both aircraft would not use more than 4G to allow for the self imposed limit on the Sabre. Even though on the surface this may not seem to truly represent the performance of either aircraft, it certainly in fact did, because both aircraft would need to employ energy preservation tactics which (as any fighter pilot will tell you) is something we always strive for, but in the heat of the fight we tend to overlook in our attempt to gain a faster kill.

Entry into the fight was from a head to head pass and I had in my mind that even though the MiG-15's power to weight ratio was inferior, the fact that we were using only 4G would help me to achieve some intimidating postures at various stages of the flight; but to my complete surprise and humility, the Sabre achieved an offensive position from only 270 degrees of a two circle fight whereupon despite my best defensive manoeuvring, he managed a guns kill in only one more turn.

Strangely enough though, the MiG-15 and Sabre's handling characteristics in the circuit are quite similar, and the landing technique for both aircraft is identical.

To give some insight into how the aircraft is operated I will briefly run through a typical display from take-off to touchdown. The take off is quite simple, the engine is run to full power on the brakes and checked for RPM 8,100, EGT (exhaust-Gas Temperature) and oil pressure within limits, fire light out etc. At this point I confirm that the nose wheel is engaged. (This is a small trap in the Sabre as you have to hold

the button in) I then release the brakes to achieve a smooth acceleration with rudder effectiveness at 50kts, rotate in the clean configuration being 120 kts. Once airborne the usual undercarriage and flaps up checks prior to 185 kts and when these are completed the RPM is reduced to 7,800 (Max Continuous power).

Prior to this demonstration I check for loose articles in the cockpit by flying upside down for a while and then execute a number of 4 G turns and reversals (the RAAF Museum Sabre is restricted to 4G for preservation purposes) to refamiliarise myself with the feel of the aircraft. At the time of run in for the display I yell to myself "It's show time!" I know that sounds rather ridiculous, but I find that it helps me to raise my concentration level and, as such, has become a habit.

The run in for the show is at an angle of about

35 degs. behind and to one side of the crowd line aiming to pass 200 yds in front of them at 60 degrees of bank to show the planform. Departure angle is the same as entry, then pulling up into a Derry turn reversal to show line at 4G. The next manoeuvre at show centre is a max rate turn at 4G and 300 kts, and this is followed by a 35 degree departure away from the crowd for another Derry turn reversal to showline. The next manoeuvre is a *twinkle* roll at show centre followed by a 35 degree departure away from the crowd and another Derry turn reversal slowing to 210kts for an open canopy run past the crowd at 100 ft. (A wave to the crowd at this point to draw attention to the open canopy) Once the canopy is closed another reposition for a 500kt pass, pulling to 45 degrees for a continuous rolling departure from the show.

It is worth noting the lack of looping manoeuvres in the show; this is for the good reason that we have seen too many historic aircraft lost from looping the aircraft into a position of 'no escape' and considering that the RAAF Museum Sabre is flown part time by both pilots, the show is kept simple and yet still should be pleasing for the public.

If the aircraft is to be returned to the venue then a 100ft, 500kt initial, with roll under fast pitch to 1,000 ft is the standard entry. Full speed brakes and 5,000 RPM into the pitch to slow the aircraft which is difficult to achieve by the base turn point. At 185 kts, gear down power 6,800 RPM to maintain 170 kts minimum. Flap (only up or down selection) is taken at the base turn point and the aircraft slowed to 150 kts min, at roll out onto finals 5,500 RPM

Cockpit of CAC Sabre A94-983/VH-PCM. Though similar to the standard CAC Sabre's cockpit, 'PCM has had a new instrument panel fitted with more modern aids, as the main role now is as a show aircraft. (James Kightly)

selected and the aircraft slowed to 130 kts aiming for a touchdown of 125 kts. The aircraft is easy to land as it sets itself down with the aid of a healthy ground effect and touchdown is generally always quite smooth even in a crosswind.

The landing roll requires effective aerodynamic braking and this is achieved by pulling the nose up until the main wheels skip slightly; the end result is a burble as the air flow finally breaks up over the wing (90 kts, aiming for this speed by 3,000 ft to run) at this stage the nose wheel is lowered to the runway and judicious braking applied. The brakes on a Sabre are

extremely powerful and there is no anti skid system, it therefore being easy to blow a tyre or aquaplane on a wet runway. Minimum runway length for our operations are 6,000 ft dry or 7,000ft wet, and although you could use less we are not prepared to put the aircraft at risk.There you have it; in summary a classic fighter with elegant lines and a crisp performance, extremely smooth to operate and slippery through the air. The turn performance is very good even at 4G and the visibility from the cockpit outstanding. (It is interesting to note that the F/A-18 canopy design is derived from the Sabre's) **WW Phil 'Frawls' Frawley.**

A94-358 / Black Diamonds, Williamtown 1961

Sqn. Ldr. Frawley has 2,200 hrs on C-130 Hercules, 800 hrs on Mirage III 0, 800 hrs F/A-18 Hornet, 800 hrs on Macchi MB 326 H with 700 as QFI. He currently holds endorsements for the Sabre, MiG-15, Hawker Sea Fury, Fiat G-59, P-40E Kittyhawk, N.A. Harvard, T-28 Trojan, B.A.C. Strikemaster and at the time of writing has been engaged to fly Australia's first MiG-21. We thank him for his contribution.

Above: An interesting addition to the piece on aerobatic teams by Adrian Balch, this CAC Sabre is from the RAAF's RED DIAMONDS aerobatic team - 76 Squadron, RAAF Williamtown AFB, New South Wales. Pictured here at Richmond on 5th February 1963 (Adrian Balch Collection)

but 'Charlie Mike is safe, and flies today regularly for the RAAF Museum, and the delight of Australian air show crowds.

The RAAF Museum, apart from having VH-PCM is fortunate in holding the prototype Sabre Mk 26, A94-101. This differs from production machines in details of the cannon armament, wing configuration and colour scheme and as a historic aircraft is rightly preserved for the future, being a natural for the *Australian Aerospace Museum* when (and if) it becomes a reality.

Complementary to the prototype the Museum also has A94-910 which is representative of the production example Mk.31 type (being converted from the Mk.30). Meanwhile at RAAF Richmond, Sabre A94-970 is under restoration to become airworthy once more, and at Wagga Wagga in store are no less than six airframes (see *Sabre Survivors* opposite).

At the quiet Victorian G.A. airfield at Morewell, where an extraordinary selection of types are hidden away, is the hangar of Jeff Trappett who apart from the well known airworthy CAC Mustang VH-AGJ and CAC Winjeel under restoration, has an Avon Sabre in dismantled state. This he aims to return to the air, and the airframe, sound, and engine mean that this is a realistic objective. Jeff, an ex RAAF pilot and current airline pilot, looks like he has an expanding number of aircraft on his hands, and naturally operates as *Latrobe Flying Museum*.

Geoff Moesker has A94-923, a composite airframe with '954's rear fuselage and currently accompanied by a spares holding of some 40 tons including the ever useful Aden cannon! At present however it looks like '923 may be sold to finance other projects, though Jeff has done a lot of research into the Sabre's past.

That is by no means the end of the Antipodean story as scattered around Australia are a large number of airframes on static display, among them A94-915 at Villawood, one of the test air-

Above: A94-101, the CAC Sabre prototype in its present configuration - still with slatted wings and gun blister (unique to this aircraft) but it now has the later type gun blast channel seen at RAAF Point Cook, in 199. (J.Kightly). Below: Unidentified CAC Sabre at Sanders Aircraft, Chino 1989 (Editor).

frames used in the trials of the Firestreak missile system before the simpler (and in many ways more effective) Sidewinder was decided upon. At Moorabin is A94-989, looking the worse for wear at present, but if their previous restorations are anything to go by it will be a stunner in the future.

Outside Australia of course the type is rarer, with examples being found in the USA, and though not normally a warbird haven, Malaya for obvious reasons. The Malay airframes are static gate guards these days though it must not be forgotten that '983 came via this route, courtesy the R.M.A.F..

In the United States is a MK.30, A94-916, owned by Charles Osborn currently after a period with *Stallion* '51 with its owner in Louisville under restoration to airworthy condition. *Sanders Aircraft* have a couple of Avon Sabres in storage pending restoration and one is close to flying. The main example is a Mk.

30, serialled A94-909, which, with assistance of the airframe of '914 should see some examples of the CAC machine to accompany and compete with the North American Aviation and Canadair variants in the skies of North America. Who knows, we may even see competitive flyoffs between the versions something which was never practicable in the Sabre's service days, and perhaps that will settle the arguments once and for all regarding the merits of each manufacturer. Whatever the conclusions there is no denying that the N.A.A. Sabre, Canadair Sabre and C.A.C. Sabre are all very fine machines indeed, whoever built them.

WW James Kightly.

Duncan & Howard Curtis list the surviving static F-86 and variant Survivors around the world in this exclusive Warbirds Worldwide Survey

Whichever way you look at it, you've really got to admit that the Sabre is one good looking aeroplane. Whether its the svelte lines of the A, E, and F, the pugnacious F-86H of the purposeful looks of the F-86D/K/L. They all look the business. And it's not surprising that close on forty air forces around the world chose the Sabre as their front line fighter;and the Sabre really lived up to those good looks. There follows an alphabetical look at the countries that flew the type, and a table of all the surviving static examples - much raw material for jet rebuilders!

Surprisingly, many Sabres are still sitting around in all corners of the globe, and some, even now, are flying operational missions more than forty years after the first example flew.

Argentina: The *Fuerza Aerea Argentina* (FAA) received 28 F-86F-30s in 1960, after an attempt to buy Canadair Sabres fell through. FAA Sabres were modified to F-40 standards prior to delivery, with the 6-3 wing, leading edge slats and 12 inches added to each wing tip. These aircraft were operated by IV Brigada Aerea, containing Gruppo de Caza-Bombardero I, II, and III. Based at El Plumerillo, FAA Sabres saw action in April 1962, when they destroyed a C-54 on the ground at Punta Indio, in the course of putting down an attempted coup. Argentine Air Force Sabres remained in service until around the late '70s, when the remaining dozen or so were first offered to Venezuela, and then Uruguay. Both these deals fell through, and the Sabres were pressed back into service with Escuadron de Caza Bombardero I

ex SAAF FSI CL-13B, Mojave 1989 (MAP)

ARGENTINA

C-	F-86F	Cordoba - EAM
C-109/52-4959	F-86F	Cordoba-ESSA/CBA - Instructional
C-111/52-4962	F-86F	Cordoba-ESSA/CBA - Instructional
'C-113'	F-86F	Mendoza, on pylon. Composite C-105/121
C-127/52-5012	F-86F	Buenos Aires Museo Nacional de Aeronautics
C-104/52-5146	F-86F	Buenos Aires, LANUS

AUSTRALIA

A94-	CA-27	Adelaide, South Australian Aviation Museum, Mundy St.
A94-922	CA-27	Amberley, Hangar 289
A94-962	CA-27	Amberley, 12 Squadron colours
A94-954	CA-27	Darwin Avn Museum, Stuart Park (also reported as 914)
A94-941	CA-27	Fisherman's Bend, CSIRO/ARL, Lorimer Street
A94-974	CA-27	RAAF Edinburgh
A94-983	CA-27	RAAF Historic Flt as VH-PCM based at Richmond
A94-942	CA-27	RAAF Kingswood, No.1 Ammunition Depot
A94-101	CA-26	Point Cook RAAF Museum
A94-901	CA-27	Mildura Airport Museum
A94-989	CA-27	Moorabin Aircraft Museum
A94-369	CA-27	Point Cook RAAF Museum, storage & restoration hangar
A94-910	CA-27	Point Cook RAAF Museum
A94-	CA-27	Point Cook RAAF Museum tail sect. & cockpit only
A94-959	CA-27	Raymond Terrace, Bettles Park, arrived August 1981
A94-923	CA-27	Toowoomba Museum.
A94-970	CA-27	RAAF Richmond, ex Wagga Wagga, rebuild to fly.
A94-982	CA-27	RAAF Wagga Wagga, gate guard

at Mendoza, in time to reinforce front-line aircraft during the Falklands/Malvinas conflict. Trials were undertaken at one point, to see if the F-86Fs could operate from the Falklands, but these ideas were soon dropped. Nonetheless, some Sabres were deployed to Comodoro Rivadavia on the eastern coast at around this time.

On 19th June, 1986, aircraft C-120 (ex-USAF 52-4963) suffered a fatigue related wing separation over Rivadavia, and crashed into a farmhouse. The pilot was killed. This led to all remaining Sabres being withdrawn from FAA service. No less than six remain in Argentina, including three at Cordoba. Aside from this, the US Air Force Academy purchased C-123 (ex USAF 52-4978) for $1, and this Sabre is on display at Colorado Springs. In 1988, Rick Sharpe at *Warbirds Unlimited*, Rosharon, Texas, bought C-111 (ex USAF 52-4962) and C-119 (ex USAF 52-5116) from the FAA, and these were registered as N7006G and N7006J respectively.

Australia: The Royal Australian Air Force had tried, unsuccessfully, to purchase US built Sabres in 1950 for service with 77Sqn in Korea. The Meteors that were purchased instead were outclassed in that conflict, and the RAAF soon realised that the Sabre was the only fighter for the job. To overcome problems of procuring North American Sabres, the Commonwealth Aircraft Company (CAC) proposed a Rolls-Royce Avon powered version of the F-86F, to be produced at their Fisherman's Bend factory. The CA-26 Sabre was thus born, though in reality, only one aircraft of this mark was made, all subsequent models being referred to as CA-27s.In order to accommodate the Avon engine, numerous modifications were required to the airframe, compared to the F-86F start point. The fuselage was deepened 3.73 inches at the intake, fairing into the fuselage contour aft of the canopy. The new engine was also mounted further aft than the J-47, and thus, the fuselage break point (for engine removal) was also moved aft. Two ADEN 30mm cannon were to provide the armament, and due to the Iso Propyl Nitrate (AvPin) starter, engine starts could be made independent of a ground power cart. In all, 268 engineering changes were made.The Commonwealth Sabre prototype first flew on 3 August 53, and the first production aircraft, the CA-27 Mk.30, flew less than a year later. In all, 111 production CAC Sabres were manufactured, the final Mk.32 having a dual store wing, uprated Avon engine (7,500 surge free pounds of thrust) and a 422 Imperial Gallons fuel capacity.

The RAAF received their first Sabre on 18 August 54, which was assigned to No.2 Operational Training Unit at Williamtown. 75 sqn became the first unit to receive the new machine, followed by numbers 3, 76, 77, and 79. Three of these squadrons served in Malaya from 1958, and RAAF Sabres of 79 sqn were also stationed at Ubon Air Base, Thailand during the Vietnam war.Final opera-

A94-907	CA-27	RAAF Wagga Wagga
A94-944	CA-27	RAAF Wagga Wagga, Technical Training School
A94-953	CA-27	RAAF Wagga Wagga, Technical Training School
A94-956	CA-27	RAAF Wagga Wagga, Technical Training School
A94-960	CA-27	RAAF Wagga Wagga, Technical Training School
A94-951	CA-27	RAAF Williamtown Museum, 3 Squadron colours
A94-915	CA-27	RAAF Villawood, Sydney.

BELGIUM
5316/52-5242	F-86F	Ex FAP. Brussells War Museum. Arrived May 1981

BOLIVIA
658	F-86F	One of six still in active service

CANADA
19101	CL13	Namao, Alberta, noted 6.90, ex Edmonton airport
23060	CL13	Sidney, BC, ex Colwood Military College
23355	CL13	Chatham RCAFB
23053	CL13	Belleville Centennial park - Golden Hawks
23649	CL13	Brockville Services Club, Ontario
23245	CL13	Peterborough as '23428', ex Clinton AFB
23651	CL13	Ottawa, National Museum of Science & Technology
23257	CL13	Trenton RCAFB, AMDU gate guard, Golden Hawks c/s
23455	CL13	Rockcliffe, national Aviation Museum
23641	CL13	Trenton, community gardens. Golden Hawks c/s
19118	CL13	Valcartier as '19430', ex St jean military college
23422	CL13	Calgary, McCall Field
23454	CL13	Calgary, McCall Field
19200	CL13	Winnipeg, RCAF MUseum, ex St Jean
23047	CL13	Oshawa airport
23221	CL13	Kingston, RMC
23301	CL13	Picton, Ontario
23228	CL13	Borden, RCAF

CHINA
F86272/52-4441	F-86F	Beijing, Museum of The Peoples' Revolution

NATIONALIST CHINA
F86098/51-2894	F-86F	Taipei, Chung Cheng aviation museum as '55065'
F86400	F-86F	location unknown

COLOMBIA
2023	CL13	Bogata, El Dorado airport

DENMARK
F-028/51-6028	F-86D	Billund Danmarks Flyvemuseum
F-947/51-5947	F-86D	Aalborg AFB, gate guard
F-421/51-8421	F-86D	Skrydstrup AFB
F- /51-	F-86D	Vaerlose AFB, Flyvevabnets Specialskole. Composite.
32 x	F-86D	At airbases as decoys, and Danish weapons ranges fates unknown

FRANCE
13-PI/55-4841	F-86K	Paris Musee de l'Air, Hall D

GERMANY
1770	CL13	Fassberg, TSLW 3
1775	CL13	Aahlhorn AB 'JA110', JG71 colours
51-13036	F-86E	Bitburg AFB, Gate Guard
1645?	CL13	Buchel, base scrapyard as wreck
1740	CL13	Fassberg TSLW 3, D9542
1784	CL13	Fassberg TSLW 3, D9523
1745	CL13	Fassberg, fire training procedures aircraft
913 ?	CL13	Furstenfeldbruck AB, fuselage BB244
1732	CL13	Goslar, Marienburgerstrasse 'GS338'
1668	CL13	Hamburg/Olsdorf Logistikschule der Bundeswehr
895	CL13	Hamburg/Olsdorf Logistikschule der Bundeswehr

tor of the CAC Sabre was 5 Operational Conversion Unit, which retired their last machines on 31st July, 1971. Many Commonwealth Sabres then found their way to the Air Forces of Indonesia and Malaysia. Two of these aircraft subsequently returned to Australia, and A94-983 (ex Malaysia) is now flying with the RAAF *Historic Flight*. The other Sabre, A94-970 (ex-Indonesian) is now being readied for flight at Richmond. The lively performance of the Avon Sabre has made it popular with collectors, and aircraft have already arrived in the USA for restoration to flying condition. Despite this, around 24 CA-26/27s remain in the country of their birth, including six at RAAF Wagga Wagga. The prototype is also preserved at the RAAF Museum, Point Cook.

Bangladesh: The Bangladesh Defence Forces/Bangladesh Biman Bahini salvaged five ex-Pakistan Air Force Canadair Sabre 6s, which were abandoned during the 24 Day War in December 1971. With the help of defecting Pakistani Air Force personnel, these aircraft were flown from Tezgaon (previously home to 14 sqn, Pakistan AF). In early 1973, 12 MiG-21MFs and 2 MiG-21Us were delivered to the BDF/BBB at Chittagong, and even though the Sabres were operated alongside the MiGs for a while, lack of spares led to the withdrawal of the remaining Mark 6s in late 1973. It is not known whether any remain in Bangladesh.

Belgium: The Forces Aerienne Belge are known to have been allocated five F-86F-25s in June, 1955. However, no details can be found of these aircraft in Belgium, and it must be assumed that they were used in trials at the time. Belgium chose the Hawker Hunter as its day fighter.

Bolivia: The Fuerza Aerea Boliviana (FAB) will probably have the distinction of being the last country to operate the Sabre as a front line fighter. The FAB received nine ex-Venezuelan AF F-86F-30s, brought up to -40 standard, in October 1973. These aircraft were operated by Brigada Aerea 21, Grupo Aerea de Caza 32 at Santa Cruz, and were supplied in natural metal finish. Overhaul work was carried out on these aircraft at the FMA facility at Cordoba in Argentina, and FAB Sabres soon had the Argentina AF-style camouflage applied. In July, 1984, two FAB F-86Fs were seriously damaged when a civilian Cessna crashed into their hangar at Santa Cruz. Around four Sabres are thought to remain in service, with the remaining survivors serving as spares sources. Due to lack of finances, it would seem that no replacement for the FAB's Sabres is likely for some time.

Burma: The Tamdaw Lay have apparently operated 12 Sabres from about 1975, though whether they are Canadair Sabre 6s or F-86Fs is not known. An educated guess would indicate that the source of these aircraft was either Thailand or Pakistan, but few other details are available. In any case, by the 1980s, Burma had lost most of its fighter

1651	CL13	Hermeskeil, Luftfahrtaustellung, as 'JA339'
1730	CL13	Jever AB on pylon as BB103
1111	CL13	Koln/Wahn, fire service
1805	CL13	Koln/Wahn, fire service
????	CL13	Koln.Wahn, noted 1978
1638	CL13	Lahr CAFB as '23444' on pylon - possibly gone Canada
1611	CL13	Lauda/Konigshofen, gate guard Tauberfrankenkaserne.
955	CL13	Manching as 'BB164'
1591	CL13	Manching, Lehrlingswerkstapp as YA005
1598	CL13	Manching as YA041
1664	CL13	Kaufbeuren TsLw1 '0106'
931	CL13	Bochum, on pylon, 'JA102'
1659	CL13	Oberschleiss heim Deutsche Aviation Museum 'KE105'
55-4897?	F-86K	Neuburg on pylon 'JD172'
55-4928	F-86K	Neuburg/Donau, JG74 barracks as 'JD119'
1715	CL13	Ottobrun, simulator with Industrie Anlagen Betriebs Gesellschaft, forward fuselage.
1746	CL13	Ottobrun, simulator with Industrie Anlagen Betriebs Gesellschaft, forward fuselage.
1813	CL13	Oldenburg AB, gate guard on pylon as JB371
1734	CL13	Oldenburg AB, gate guard on pylon as JB110
840	CL13	Pinneberg, Eggerstedt Kaserne, JB 111
1814	CL13	Pferdsfeld, JaBoG 35 gate guard as JC102
838	CL13	Roth, barracks 'JA130'
1696	CL13	Rottenburg, FlaRakBtl 34 as JC101
52-5372	F-86F	Sembach AFB, gate guard
1605	CL13	Sollingen, gate guard
1613	CL13	Sinsheim 'YA042'
819	CL13	Sonthofen, Jagerkaserne BB112
801	CL13	Uetersen, Luftwaffe Museum BB150
1643	CL13	Uetersen, Luftwaffe Museum JB110
1603	CL13	Uetersen, Luftwaffe Museum D9539
55-4881	F-86K	Uetersen, Luftwaffe Museum JD249
	CL13	Uetersen, Luftwaffe Museum see 895
1625	CL13	Wittmundhafen, JA111
1724	CL13	Wittmundhafen, Fliegerkaserne JA112

GREECE

51-8404 (?)	F-86D	Athens War Museum as '16171'
	CL13	Thessaloniki/Mikra preserved at aero club '19494'
19168	CL13	Thessaloniki/Mikra
	CL13	Thessaloniki/Mikra reported as '19237'
19347	CL13	Thessaloniki/Mikra
	CL13	Thessaloniki/Mikra reported as '19198'
19448	CL13	Nea Ankhialos, on display
3 x	F-86	Larissa AB as decoys
51-6149	F-86D	Previza AFB on dump
51-8297	F-86D	Previza AFB on dump
51-8404 (?)	F-86D	Previza AFB on dump
51-6182	F-86D	Araxos AFB as decoy
51-8392	F-86D	Araxos AFB as decoy
	F-86?	Andravida AFB as gate guard
	F-86?	Tanagra, reported as '52235'

HONDURAS

	F-86K	La Ceiba, derelict
	F-86K	San Pedro Sula
	F-86K	San Pedro Sula
	CL-13	San Pedro Sula
	CL-13	San Pedro Sula
FAH-100	F-86K	Tegucigalpa Airport, preserved by December 1986

INDIA

| 52-5248 | F-86F | Palam, Indian Air Force Museum. PAF wreckage |

INDONESIA

| 8611/A94-971 | CA27 | Bandung, PT Nurtanio factory |

Top: Resplendent in its Golden Hawks paint scheme Canadair CL-13 serial 23257 is displayed at Trenton CAFB (Duncan Curtis) **Lower:** *Not looking so good is the remains of F-86K 51-56, ex Italian AF, and actually 55-4869 at Castrette, Perimetals Scrapyard in 1987 (MAP)*

capability.

Canada: The Canadians were the first to take out a licence to build the Sabre. The Canadair CL-13 was assembled at Cartierville, near Montreal, and in all, 1815 Canadian Sabres rolled of the production line. The CL-13 Mk.1 was basically a Canadian built F-86A, whilst the Mk.2 and 4 were equivalent to the F-86E. However, by fitting the Canadian Orenda engine to the Mks 5 and 6, an aircraft

8614/A94-980	CA-27	Bandung, PT Nurtanio factory
	CA-27	Bandung, PT Nurtanio factory
8615/A94-988	CA-27	HQ Training Command Museum (location?)
8618	CA-27	Jog Jakarta, Indonesian AF Museum
8622	CA-27	Pekanbaru
ITALY		
19534	CL13	Turin/Caselle, preserved by AMI
53-8303	F-86K	Gioia del Colle, gate guard
55-4863	F-86K	Istrana as '38276', coded 51-01

resulted that had a distinct 'edge' over U.S.-built F-86Fs. The Royal Canadian Air Force (RCAF) received their first Sabres into 410 Sqn. at Dorval in April, 1951, and from November, 1951, RCAF Sabres were stationed in Europe. Ultimately, thirteen front line RCAF squadrons received the type, plus six Auxiliary Squadrons. The last unit to use the Sabre in RCAF was the Sabre Transition Unit at Chatham, which replaced it's last aircraft in November 1968. Twenty or so remain in Canada, including the first Canadair Sabre, 9101, which is preserved at Namao, Alberta, having previously been displayed at Edmonton Airport for a number of years. Additionally, the Canadair Sabre has proved very popular with civilian operators, from Mojave-based *Flight Systems* to the *Combat Jets Flying Museum*. In all, around 84 Canadair Sabres were entered on the U.S. Civil Aircraft Register (mainly due to U.S.-built Sabres being 'de-milled' at the end of their service life), plus seven in Canada, one in West Germany and one in the UK.

Colombia: The Fuerza Aerea Colombiana (FAC) bought six brand new Canadair Sabre 6s at a cost of $500,000 each. These were deliv-

53-8299	F-86K	Gallarate, 2 Deposito Centrale, coded 51-6
53-8291	F-86K	Rimini AB, gate guard coded 5-53
55-4868	F-86K	Vigna di Valle AMI Museum, coded 51-62
19782	CL13	Pisa Technical School coded 4-83
19724	CL13	Rivolto AB, Frecce Tricolori c/s
19668	CL13	Cameri AB, Lanceri Neri c/s, parts of 19509
19523	CL13	Grazzanise, tail of 19664 ex Capua/Rivolto
53-8297	F-86K	Capua, Scuola Specialiti AM coded 51-60
	F-86K	Aviano, town centre, on pylon as 63-8189
53-8274	F-86K	Alessandria, Instituto tecnico Volta, coded 5-57
55-4812	F-86K	Milan, Museo Alfa Romeo di Arese, coded 51-3
19664	CL13	Capua, Scuola Specialisti AM, Cavallino Rampante c/s
19666	CL13	Rome, Instituto Galileo Galilei
19723	CL13	Rivolto Air base
19792	CL13	Vigna di Valle, AMI Museum
19841	CL13	Grosseto AB
19596	CL13	Caserta, AMI NCO school coded 4-46
54-1292	F-86K	Rivolto AB Museum, tail of 55-4818
53-8316	F-86K	Cameri AB, Gruppo Hangar coded 51-21
55-4869	F-86K	Castrette scrapyard coded 51-56
55-4858	F-86K	Castrette scrapyard coded 51-51
54-1288	F-86K	Castrette scrapyard coded 51-72
54-1256	F-86K	Castrette scrapyard
53-8300	F-86K	Vizzola Ticino, Caproni Museum coded 5-55

JAPAN

84-8103/51-8375	F-86D	Iruma AB

Above: ex Japanese RF-86F 62-7416 at China Lake, 1989. Used for spares for QF-86Fs at China Lake, it is probably not still extant! (MAP)

ered on 8th June 1956, and equipped No.1 Escuadron de Caza Bombardero at Germán Olano Air Base near Bogota. These aircraft replaced F-47D Thunderbolts in the fighter bomber rôle. Two ex-Spanish Air Force F-86Fs arrived in January 1963 to replace aircraft lost in accidents. It is thought that two Sabres of each model were left when withdrawal came in 1966. One Canadair Sabre remains in Colombia: serial 2023 at Bogota.

82-7807/51-8375	F-86D	Iruma AB
84-8104/52-4042	F-86D	Hamamatsu AB
72-7749/55-5096	F-86F	Hamamatsu/Mianmi ground school, Blue Impulse c/s
02-7960/57-6417	F-86F	Hamamatsu gate guard
02-7966/57-6423	F-86F	Hamamatsu
52-7406/52-4845	F-86F	Ashiya AB
52-7408/51-13376	F-86F	Komatsu AB
62-7415/52-4916	F-86F	Chitose AB
62-7427/52-4909	F-86F	Gifu AB, gate guard
62-7527/55-3929	F-86F	Nara City Officers School
62-7508/55-3925	F-86F	Misawa AB, outside 432TFW USAF HQ
62-7516/55-3891	F-86F	Shimizu

Top: *F-86F Sabre, 92-7894 of the JASDF Blue Impulse display team seen taxying at Tsuiki Air Base in November 1973. Several survivors in Japan wear this scheme (Adrian Balch Collection)*

Denmark: The Royal Danish Air Force (RDAF)/Kongelige Dankse Flyvevabnet received 59 F-86Ds which were mainly ex-USAFE. The first 38 were delivered from 26 June 1958, with the remaining 21 following in 1960. A further three F-86Ds were bought in March 1962 for spares use. In common with a number of other European Sabre operators, the RDAF modified many of their F-86Ds to accept the superior Martin Baker Mk.5 ejector seat. These machines served with Eskadrille 723 and 726 at Aalborg, and 728 at Skydstrup, being phased out on 31 March 1966 in favour of the CF-104G Starfighter. Though 20 RDAF F-86Ds were written off in service, the majority of the survivors went on to serve as decoys at the airfields of Karup, Aalborg, Skydstrup and Vandel. In 1988-89, around thirty were still in existence, but at about this time, some were scrapped, whilst others were sent to the ranges at Oksbol. It is known that some do still survive however. North East Air Museum at Sunderland , UK has been lucky to receive RDAF parts for the restoration of their F-86D, and currently, three Sabres are preserved in Denmark.

Ethiopia: The Imperial Ethiopian Air Force/*Ye Ityopya Ayer Hayl* received twelve F-86F-30s in July 1960. These went to equip Ethiopia's first interceptor squadron. At this time, IEAF had a strength of around 4,500 personnel and was supervised by both Swedish and US instructors. It is thought that other F-86Fs were purchased at a later date, possibly form Iran. Ultimately, 25 Sabres were placed in IEAF service at their base at Debre

62-7702/55-5049	F-86F	Komaki, Mitsubishi factory
72-7727/55-5074	F-86F	Tosu/Saga
82-7778/56-2780	F-86F	Komaki airport
72-7708/55-5055	F-86F	Shishiku
82-7818/56-2820	F-86F	Utsonamiya
92-7885/57-6342	F-86F	Hiyakuri AB
92-7905/57-6362	F-86F	Tosu/Saga
92-7922/57-6379	F-86F	Tsuiki AB
92-7929/57-6386	F-86F	Hamamatsu/Kita AB gate guard
92-7938/57-6395	F-86F	Tsuiki AB gate guard
02-7946/57-6403	F-86F	Namerikawa
84-8102/51-8344	F-86D	Kisarazu
84-8105/51-5858	F-86D	Shizuoka
84-8106/51-5957	F-86D	Ashiya AB
84-8109/51-6002	F-86D	Toritsu Industrial College
84-8112/51-6033	F-86D	Tomakomai
84-8113/51-6042	F-86D	Utsonamiya
84-8114/51-6080	F-86D	Takasuki
84-8115/51-6086	F-86D	Tsuiki AB
04-8183/52-3979	F-86D	Shizuhama AB
94-8125/51-5992	F-86D	Komaki/Nagoya airport on Terminal roof
84-8117/51-6098	F-86D	Tokyo
84-8118/51-2169	F-86D	Nemuro
84-8119/51-6132	F-86D	Chitose AB
84-8124/51-5974	F-86D	Kisarazu
84-8126/51-6013	F-86D	Jinmachi JGSDF
84-8127/51-5967	F-86D	Hofu South AB
84-8128/51-5989	F-86D	Kumagaya, 4th technical school
84-8131/51-6040	F-86D	Asahikawa
94-8132/51-6066	F-86D	Tochigi
94-8133/51-5982	F-86D	Timioka
81-8134/51-5986	F-86D	Matsushima AB
94-8138/51-5973	F-86D	Kumamoto
94-8139/51-6104	F-86D	Tokyo
84-8145/51-5912	F-86D	Fukouka
94-8146/51-6023	F-86D	Omimura - Hijiri Museum
84-8150/51-6003	F-86D	Fukushima
94-8153/51-5988	F-86D	Tsuchiura
84-8157/51-5991	F-86D	Saga Chuo Industrial High School
04-8162/51-6166	F-86D	Kumamoto

ebit. These aircraft fought in the war with
omalia in 1978-79, by which time only a
ozen were left in flying condition. Much
peculation exists as to service beyond these
ates, but Sabres were still present at Debre
ebit as late as February 1986. Their exact
tatus then and now is unknown.

France: The French Air Force/Armée de l'Air
eceived 60 Fiat-built F-86Ks between August
956 and June 1957. One other aircraft, 55-
880, was allocated but not delivered. ECTT
/13 *Artois* received their first Sabres at Lahr
n September 1956, before moving to Colmar,
vhilst ECTT 2/13 *Alpes* formed at Colmar in
May 1957. When the first Mirages arrived in
962, ECTT 1/13 passed their F-86Ks to the
lpes squadron, and they in turn passed their
emaining Sabres to a newly-formed unit,
/13, in April 1962. 22 French F-86Ks were
eturned to Italy by July 1962, and the final
ircraft were withdrawn in August of that year.
nder orders of MAP, the majority of the
emaining aircraft were destroyed in France,
nding their days at Chateauroux. Only one
ircraft survived, 55-4841, which was pre-
erved on the gate at Colmar for many years,
ut is now safely with the *Museum de l'Air*.

Greece: The Greek Air Force/*Elliniki Polmiki
Aeroporia* operated both the Canadair Sabre
and the F-86D from the mid fifties. The first
f 104 Canadair Sabres arrived in 1954 and
tarted to equip the newly formed 341 Day

*elow: Located at Basa Air Force Base in the
hilippines is F-86F serial 52-5158 which is
ecurely mounted on a pylon in poor condi-
on. There are at least four other Sabres out
ere in varying condition. (MAP)*

04-8164/51-6200	F-86D	Nara
04-8171/51-8275	F-86D	Komatsu
04-8175/52-3920	F-86D	Tokushima
04-8177/52-3969	F-86D	Niigata
04-8178/52-3949	F-86D	Fukui Airport
04-8181/52-3972	F-86D	Okayama
04-8184/52-3984	F-86D	Chiba
04-8185/52-3885	F-86D	Hamamatsu
04-8187/52-4013	F-86D	Nyutabaru AB
04-8191/52-10014	F-86D	Zuntsuji
04-8192/52-10093	F-86D	Wakkanai
04-8194/52-10119	F-86D	Mie
04-8195/52-9998	F-86D	Kaimon Shizen Park
82-7849/56-2851	F-86D	Kumagaya, 4th technical School
04-8196/52-10003	F-86D	Nara
04-8197/52-4071	F-86D	Hiyakuri AB
04-8199/52-4105	F-86D	Chitose AB
04-8200/52-4024	F-86D	Fukushima, Banko Paradise
04-8202/52-4045	F-86D	Miho AB
04-8203/52-4301	F-86D	Hofu North AB
04-8204/52-9987	F-86D	Chiba
84-8111/51-6030	F-86D	Komaki AB
04-8205/52-9989	F-86D	Yamanashi, Nihon Koku Gakuen
04-8209/52-10000	F-86D	Gifu AB, gate guard
14-8217/52-3966	F-86D	Komatsu AB
14-8222/52-10103	F-86D	Ohtsu
52-4341	F-86F	Kadena AFB, Okinawa (USAF serial)
84-8101/51-8368	F-86D	Kofu, Maizuru park
04-8176/52-3898	F-86D	Nagoya Municipal Science Museum
72-7743/55-5090	F-86F	Aichi - preserved in park
82-7789/56-2791	F-86F	Matsushima AB
82-7865/56-2867	F-86F	Omimura, Hijiri Museum
92-7888/57-6345	F-86F	Oita Heiwa Koen
92-7919/57-6376	F-86F	Hamamatsu AB
02-7951/57-6408	F-86F	Yahatahama, Kanko Centre
82-7808/56-2810	F-86F	Hamamatsu AB
52-7402/51-13474	F-86F	Tokyo Airport

MAP

Top: This ex Portuguese AF F-86F is at the Brussels War Museum. The Portuguese have several more in store serial;5316 / 52-5242

Fighter squadron. In 1955, further Sabres equipped 342 and 343 squadrons at Elefsina. In 1956, the fighter squadrons transferred to Tanagra where they were based until around 1966, when surviving aircraft were placed in storage. F-86Ds were bought in 1960, and the first of 35 arrived on 17th May that year. The first squadron to equip was 337, and on 12th May 1961, 343 squadron received their first F-86D and operated until November 1965. 337 squadron replaced their Sabres in May 1967. The Greek A.F. replaced their Sabres with a mixture of F-104G Starfighters and F-5As. A number of F-86Ds were used as decoys in their retirement, and some still exist, as well as a fair number of preserved CL-13 Mk.2s

Honduras: A mixture of Sabres was operated by the *Fuerza Aerea Hondurena*. Eight ex-Yugoslav Air Force (and prior to that, ex-RAF) Sabre 4s were supplied from Fort Lauderdale, Florida, where they had arrived in crates. The Sabres were assembled in a warehouse on the north side of the airfield and towed down the road to the active ramp. These aircraft were then flown to San Pedro Sula in Honduras at the rate of one aircraft every two weeks, starting in the spring of 1976. Here they were operated by Escuadron Sabre, being supplemented by around 4 F-86Fs which arrived in 1977. In 1969, five F-86Ks were purchased from Venezuela, and these machines may have flown against El Salvadorian aircraft after the end of the infamous 'Soccer War'. These aircraft served until around 1980. The CL-13s and F-86Fs were

52-7405/52-4705	F-86F	Shizuoka, Nihon Daira Yuenchi
52-7403/52-4618	F-86F	Hofu South AB

REPUBLIC OF KOREA
51-6245	F-86D	Suwon AFB, gate guard
51-13180	F-86F	Seoul War Museum, May 16th Plaza
51-8424	F-86D	Seoul War Museum
52-5429	F-86F	Possibly still in service
52-4865	F-86F	Possibly still in service, Taegu
52-4874	RF-86F	ditto
12910	F-86F	Osan AFB

MALAYSIA
FM1900	CA27	Kinara, RMAF School of Aeronautical Engineering
FM1905	CA27	Butterworth AFB, gate guard
FM1904	CA27	Sungai Besi Museum
FM1907	CA27	Sungai Besi Museum

NETHERLANDS
52-5180	F-86F	Militar Luchtvaart Museum. Ex FAP 5307
Q-283/54-1283	F-86K	Twenthe AFB gate guard on pylon
1704	CL13	Budel Army Barracks as JC-240 ex Luftwaffe
53-8305	F-86K	Militar Luchtvaart Museum. Ex Italian AF

NORWAY
54-1290	F-86K	Gardermoen AFB, 335 Skv area on pylon coded ZK-Z
53-1206	F-86F	Gardermoen AFB, RNo AF Museum
54-1313	F-86K	Gardermoen AFB, ex Bardufoss
52-5069	F-86F	Gardermoen AFB, RNoAF Museum
53-1220	F-86F	Lista AFB
54-1274	F-86K	Oslo Air Mechanics School. On loan from RNoA Museum
52-5202	F-86F	Orland, ex Gardermoen
53-1082	F-86F	Gardermoen AFB, R No AF Museum
54-1215	F-86K	Gardermoen AFB, RNoAF Museum
54-1266	F-86K	Flyhistorisk Museum, Stavanger/Sola.
54-1245	F-86K	Oslo/Arkhus, ex Bodo, coded RI-Z

till in use in 1986, when they were replaced by Dassault Mystères, though the Sabres were not broken up immediately, and it is thought that a number survive. It would be nice to see at least one fly again, maybe even in the colour scheme it wore whilst with the RAF. One F-86K is also preserved at Tegucigalpa airport.

Indonesia: The *Tentara Nasional Indonesia-Angkatan Udara* (TNI-AU) was given 16 CAC Sabre 32s in April 1972. The first of these aircraft arrived on 19th February, 1973 from Australia, the final machines following on the 1st. Five more ex Malaysian AF CA-27s arrived in 1976. TNI-AU Sabres were initially operated by 14 squadron, but in a redesignation in 1974, the unit was renamed the SAT SERGAP F-86 squadron. It is understood that remaining aircraft were replaced in the 1980s, when the country received Northrop F-5s and General Dynamics F-16s. A good number are still extant in Indonesia, and one aircraft has returned to Australia for return to flying condition.

Iran: The Imperial Iranian Air Force (IIAF) operated a number of F-86Fs until the early 1970s, these aircraft also flying with the aerobatic team *Golden Crown*, before F-5s replaced them. Exact dates are not known at present, and it is doubtful if Sabres exist in this part of the world. In 1966, Iran gained

Below: An FAV F-86F 1A36 at Maracay on 5th November 1992. Note wheel clamps which keep the aircraft tyres off the floor (Gerry Manning photograph)

PAKISTAN

53-1163	F-86F	Risalpur AFB, gate guard
51-13315	F-86F	Kamra AFB for preservation
53-1125	F-86F	Chaklala AFB
51-13447	F-86F	Sargodha AFB, gate guard
55-5005	F-86F	Peshawar AFB, gate guard
55-3850	F-86F	Karachi/faisal AFB, gate guard
53-1176	F-86F	Korangi Creek AFB, gate guard
1595	CL13	Masroor AFB, decoy
1629	CL13	Masroor AFB, decoy
1705	CL13	Masroor AFB, decoy
1739	CL13	Masroor AFB, decoy
1764	CL13	Masroor AFB, decoy
1815	CL13	Masroor AFB, decoy. Last Canadair Sabre built
1747	CL13	Karachi/Faisal AFB, PAF Workshops
1794	CL13	Karachi/Faisal AFB, PAF Workshops
1632	CL13	Karachi/Faisal AFB, on pylon.
1810	CL13	Korangi Creek AFB, gate guard
1670	CL13	Lahore
1728	CL13	Lahore
1754	CL13	Masroor AFB, base school
1789	CL13	Masroor, College.

PHILIPPINES

51-8436	F-86D	Basa AFB, gate guard
52-4468	F-86F	Villamor AFB
52-10015	F-86D	Villamor AFB, gate guard
52-4428	F-86F	Basa AFB, "Budjak"
52-5158	F-86F	Basa AFB, on pylon.

PORTUGAL

5344/52-5267	F-86F	Cascais/Tires airport, all white.
5319/52-5262	F-86F	Ota Technical School
5301/52-5168	F-86F	Monte Real, gate guard on pylon
5320/52-5268	F-86F	Monte Real Museum, airworthy condition.

notoriety for acting as the middle man in Pakistan's purchase of 90 ex-Luftwaffe Sabre 6s. Though the aircraft were flown to Iran, supposedly for service with IIAF, they then passed on to Pakistan ostensibly for overhaul, but never returned. Pakistan was subject to a UN arms embargo at the time.

Iraq: The Iraqis received five F-86Fs in 1958, the first aircraft of a larger order. However, after the overthrow of King Faisal II in July of the same year, the US vetoed any further arms shipments. It is doubtful that these aircraft saw much service, but any information concerning their use would be very interesting.

Italy: The Aeronautica Militare Italiana (AMI) operated both ex-RAF Sabre 4s and Fiat-built F-86Ks. First of 180 Sabre 4s arrived from the UK in 1956 and served with seven Gruppi until replaced by Fiat G-91s and F-86Ks from 1960. In 1962, five AMI Sabre 4s were sent to the Congo as part of the UN effort, where they were flown by Philippine AF pilots. One of these aircraft remained, and can be seen at Kinshasa University in Zaire. Fiat produced 221 F-86Ks under licence at it's Turin/Caselle plant, and 93 of these flew with the AMI, whilst others went to France, West Germany and Norway. The first Fiat F-86K flew on 23rd May 1955, and soon these aircraft were equipping Gruppi 6, 17 and 23. The last AMI aircraft was delivered on 31st October 1957, though other F-86Ks augmented Italian AF aircraft when Holland (US-built F-86Ks) and France returned Sabres in the early 1960s. 12, 21 and 22 Gruppi later received the F-86K when 6 and 17 Gruppi became missile units. The final F-86K flight in AMI was flown by Captain Mario Pinna in 53-8291 on 27 July 1973, with 23 Gruppo at Rimini. Total hours flown by the F-86Ks was 162,396.00. Many Sabres still remain in Italy (and one CL13 Mk.4 is due to return to the UK, for eventual display at the RAF Museum)

Japan: The Japanese Air Self Defence Force (JASDF) operated 435 F-86Fs and 122 F-86Ds, making Japan the third largest user of the type. Initially, 180 F-86Fs were received from the U.S. from December 1955 to early 1957, though due to a shortage of pilots, the last 45 were returned to the United States. Mitsubishi built another 300 F-86Fs between 1956 and 1961, and also converted 18 of the U.S. supplied batch to RF-86F photo recce aircraft from 1961. JASDF F-86Fs served with squadrons (Hikotai) 1 to 10 as well as the famous Blue Impulse aerobatic team. Thirty F-86Fs were stored at 2nd Air Depot at Gifu, and the last of these arrived in 1967. After work, which included fitting the fuselage of a retired airframe, these 'as new' F-86Fs were re-activated between 1976 and 1979, assuming the identity of the wings of the mothballed aircraft! The last JASDF F-86F flight was on 15th March 1982, by 62-7497 (previously USAF 55-3937) of HQ Squadron at Iruma. From January 1958, the JASDF gained an all weather fighter capability with the arrival of the first F-86Ds. These went to serve with

5333/52-5184	F-86F	Alverca Museu do Ar store
5337/52-5199	F-86F	Alverca Museu do Ar store
5338/52-5204	F-86F	Alverca Museu do Ar store
5347/53-1083	F-86F	Alverca Museu do Ar store
5360/53-1190	F-86F	Alverca Museu do Ar store
12 x F-86Fs		Sintra Scrapyard

SAUDI ARABIA

713/	F-86F	Dharan AFB, Technical Training Institute
709 ?/52-4537	F-86F	Dharan AFB, gate guard, on pylon
715	F-86F	Dharan AFB, scrap area
'1512'	F-86F	Dharan AFB, scrap area
705/53-1122	F-86F	Dharan AFB, Technical Training Institute
701/52-5136	F-86F	Dharan AFB, scrap area
702/	F-86F	Dharan AFB, scrap area
703/53-1089	F-86F	Dharan AFB, scrap area
704	F-86F	Dharan AFB, scrap area
706	F-86F	Dharan AFB, scrap area
716/52-5278	F-86F	Dharan AFB, scrap area
720/52-4497	F-86F	Dharan AFB, scrap area
/53-1072	F-86F	Dharan AFB, scrap area

SOUTH AFRICA

361	CL13	Swartkop AFB, displayed in Korean War colours
372	CL13	Ysterplaat AFB
367	CL13	Swartkop AB
358	CL13	Pieterburg
369	CL13	Waterkloof AFB
383	CL13	Kempton Park Technical College

SPAIN

C5-5/51-13125	F-86F	Valencia AFB (Manises) coded 1-005
C5-71/52-4718	F-86F	Villa Nova ex Cuatro Vientos
C5-223/51-13450	F-86F	Museo del Aire, Cuatro Vientos as 'C5-104'
C5-58/52-4594	F-86F	Museo de Aire, Cuatro Vientos coded 102-4
C5-231/52-5307	F-86F	Moron AFB, coded 151-21
C5-1/51-13194	F-86F	Leon AFB, Virgen del Camino Technical Training Scool
C5-107/55-3981	F-86F	Leon AFB, Virgen del Camino TTS, coded 131-8
C5-82/55-3966	F-86F	Torrejon AFB, ala 12 area
C5-2/51-13239	F-86F	Talavera la Real AFB, gate guard as C5-199/732-1
C5-70/52-4683	F-86F	Zaragoza AFB, on pylon
C5-143/55-3971	F-86F	Zaragoza AFB, gate guard USAF Korean c/s as 25406
34 x F-86Fs		Las Bardenas weapons ranges

THAILAND

4322/52-5060	F-86F	Bangkok, Thai AF Museum
1215/53-681	F-86L	Bangkok, Thai AF Museum
	F-86	Thai AF School
1214/53-677	F-86L	Don Muang AFB
1232/53-892	F-86L	Don Muang AFB, Thai AF Academy
1315/52-5022	F-86F	Don Muang AFB, gate guard, ex TAF Academy
1314/51-13220	F-86F	Possibly at Don Muang
4335/52-5044	F-86F	Possibly at Don Muang
1213/53-626	F-86L	Bangkok, Liumpini park, ex Thai AF School
2001/	F-86F	Lop Buri AFB, gate guard
4321/51-13232	F-86F	Takhli, town centre

TURKEY

19207	CL13	Ataturk, Turkish AF Museum
19268	CL13	Ataturk, Turkish AF Museum
19103	CL13	Murted AB, on pylon in White Swan's colours

UNITED KINGDOM

XB733/G-ATBF	CL13	Ex Dandy's farm. Sold, location unknown

01,102,103 and 105 *Hikotais* and the last aircraft were withdrawn in October 1968. Many SDF F-86Fs were returned to the U..SA., nder the terms of the MAP for use in the U.S. avy's QF-86F drone programme. Many abres still live on in Japan, both F and D mods, but presumably they are still nominally on SDF charge, as the U.S. funded aircraft are upposed to be either scrapped, bought or turned to the US on retirement.

Yugoslavia: The *Jugoslavensko Ratno azduhplovstvo* (JRV) was another country hich used ex-RAF Sabre 4s, in this case 121 ere supplied from 1956. These aircraft were alled F-86E(M) after overhaul in the UK. JRV abres were based at Batajnacica near elgrade, and indeed, it was a Sabre 4 flown y Colonel Nikola Lekic which broke the ound barrier for the first time in Yugoslavia n July 31st 1956. Around 130 ex-USAF F-5Ds were obtained in 1961, and though abre 4s were replaced in the mid 70s, the D odel served until at least 1980, when there ere 20 or so in service at Skopje. There are abres of both variants preserved at the JRV useum in Belgrade, as well as F-86Ds at ubljana and Zagreb Airports, though the former is possibly no longer extant after military ction at the location. One other-JRV F-86D as seen in the United States in 1987: 14024 RV serial) was in the yard of *Hurrican* *ucking* at Pasadena Texas but has not been eard of since.

Republic of Korea: The Republic of Korea r Force (ROKAF) received the first of 85 86Fs in 1955, from the USAF. Twenty Seven ther aircraft were purchased in 1958, and ound ten of the total were to RF-86F con-guration. Other MAP aircraft followed at ter dates, and it is known that at least one -Spanish AF F-86F served with ROKAF. The 86Fs served with two day fighter wings, con-ining three squadrons each. In November 960, the first of 40 F-86Ds arrived, and went n to equip the ROKAFs first all weather inter-ptor squadron. By 1978/9, the remaining 86Ds were retired, and many of the 50-odd 86Fs were also withdrawn, but it is fairly cer-in that at least three F-86Fs remained in ring condition at Taegu until 1987. Some OKAF F-86Fs have been returned to the US r use at China Lake, but so far, only two or ree have been converted to QF-86F config-ation. Over in Oregon, the *Military Museum* Clackamas imported an ex-ROKAF F-86F in 984. Four Sabres are known to be preserved South Korea.

Malaysia: Malaysia was the first export stomer for the Australian CAC Sabre. The yal Malaysian Air Force/*Tentara Udara iraja Malaysia* (RMAF/TUDM) was given ten abre 32s by the Australian Government in pril 1969. These aircraft arrived in Malaysia October of the same year, and were fol-wed up by another six aircraft in 1971. dditionally, two non flying machines were pplied as training aids. 11 Squadron oper-

51-6171	F-86D	Sunderland, North East Air Museum ex Greek AF

UNITED STATES

Alabama

52—4243	F-86D	Birmingham
53-973	F-86L	Montgomery, Highway 80
53-847	F-86D	Montgomery, Highway 80
53-806	F-86D	Maxwell AFB
53-566	F-86D	Montgomery, George Washington Carver High School
49-1301	F-86A	Maxwell AFB as '12760'
51-2993	F-86D	Mobile, USS Alabama Memorial Park

Alaska

49-1195	F-86A	Kulis ANG base, Alaska ANG Museum

Arizona

52-2095	F-86H	Ajo, American legion Post
53-808	F-86L	Tucson International airport
51-6261	F-86L	Chandler City Park as '210115'
51-5915	F-86D	San Carlos, on pylon, ex Globe
51-13371	F-86F	Champlin Fighter Museum, Mesa
52-5323	F-86F	Luke AFB collection
55-3818	F-86F	Phoenix Skyharbor, Arizona ANG Collection
53-763	F-86D	Phoenix, Goodyear Field
53-1525	F-86H	Tucson, Pima County Air Museum
53-965	F-86L	Tucson, Pima County Air Museum
139531	FJ4B	Tucson, Pima County Air Museum
52-2844/19263	CL13	Williams AFB, gate guard
51-6071	F-86D	Davis Monthan AFB ex N86RJ and N3280U

Arkansas

52-3653	F-86D	Little Rock AFB collection, camp Robinson
53-1047	F-86D	Wilson. Possibly scrapped

California

53-563	F-86D	Alhambra. Possibly scrapped
51-3012	F-86D	Auburn
51-13067	F-86E	Banning airport
51-6056	F-86D	Beale AFB Collection
51-2998	F-86D	Blythe. Possibly scrapped
53-1230	F-86H	Castle AFB Museum as Bernie's Bo
53-903	F-86D	Chico. Possibly scrapped
14 x F-86Ls		China Lake NAS Ranges
53-994	F-86L	Rosamund, El Dorado Aircraft Supplies, ex Reno
'313'	FJ3	Planes of Fame, Chino
49-1217	F-86A	Planes of Fame, Chino as '91318'
48-242	F-86A	Planes of Fame, Chino
53-1351	QF-86H	Planes of Fame, Chino
53-1357	F-86H	Planes of Fame, Chino
23504	CL13	Chino, ex Mesa
135883	FJ3	El Toro MCAS on loan from Quantico as '136022'
51-2950	F-86D	Dixon Possibly scrapped
53-642	F-86D	Fresno ANG Collection
49-1272	F-86A	Fresno ANG Collection, Ole Leroy
	F-86L	Hawthorne, Western Museum of Flight
53-703	F-86D	Lompoc/Arroyo Grande - possibly scrapped.
53-1238	F-86H	Long beach Airport
53-1304	F-86H	March AFB
51-13082	F-86E	McLellan AFB Collection ex Gaviota/Vista Del Mar sch.
51-2968	F-86L	McLellan AFB Collection. ex Mercedes, TX
52-5241	F-86F	Edwards AFB Flight Test history museum
53-1515	F-86H	George AFB, Wing HQ ex San Bernadino
53-3682	F-86D	Mill valley/Santa Cruz
23323	CL13	Mojave, fire dump
N186F	CL13	Mojave, Fire dump
52-10170	F-86D	Montclair

ated these aircraft from Butterworth until 1975-6 when they were replaced with F-5A and Bs. At this time, 12 squadron was formed, and operated the remaining aircraft until later in 1976. Apart from the aircraft remaining in Malaysia, in 1978, one RMAF Sabre, A94-983/FM1983, was transported back to Australia, and this aircraft now flies with the RAAF *Historic Flight*.

Netherlands: *Koninklijke Luchtmacht* (Klu) received the first of 57 U.S. built F-86Ks by sea in October 1955. The last arrived in April 1957. Six Fiat F-86Ks also arrived in April/May of 1957. Three squadrons operated the F-86K; 701 and 702 at Twenthe, and 700 at Soesterburg, though by 1960, all KLu Sabres were based at Twenthe. Interestingly, the KLu transferred personnel to Soesterburg in 1955 to commence training pilots and navigators on the expected (two-seat) all weather fighter. In the end , as the F-86K had been chosen, there were a lot of redundant navigators.KLu phased out the F-86K in June 1964 having already sent back 8 aircraft to Italy in 1963. The majority of the survivors were then scrapped, though two Sabres escaped-54-1283/Q-283, which was preserved at Twenthe, and 54-1296 which went to Kouderkerk, but was scrapped at a later date. In 1973, the Dutch required an F-86K for display at the museum at Soesterburg, and since all KLu Sabres had long since been scrapped, the Italian Air Force kindly made a gift to the Dutch. Thus, 53-8305 was flown from Rimini to Deelen, Holland on 10 June 1973, resplendent in it's new KLu colours as Q-305.

Norway: The Royal Norwegian Air Force (RNoAF) replaced their F-84G Thunderjets

Below: The world's oldest F-86:47-605, Lackland, Texas (MAP)

Serial	Type	Location
52-4159	F-86D	Morro Bay
52-2102	F-86H	Novato
52-2054	F-86H	Palmdale, Plant 42
51-8415	F-86D	Paso Robles/Shandon
52-5459	F-86F	Redding Possibly scrapped
53-914	F-86D	Rialto
53-1380	F-86H	Rialto
	CL13	San Diego Aerospace Museum
23238	CL13	Van Nuys outside CA ANG hangar as '12910'
53-1160	F-86F	Rio Linda
52-2074	F-86H	Riverside, derelict
53-704	F-86L	Travis AFB
49-1248	F-86A	San Bernardino Possibly scrapped
51-13037	F-86E	Norton AFB
132115	FJ2	Carl Larsen park, San Francisco
53-1399	F-86H	Truckee, on pylon derelict
53-997	F-86L	Butte, on pylon as City of Butte
352	CL13	Mojave, Flight Systems, stored ex SAAF, N38301
359	CL13	Mojave, Flight Systems, stored ex SAAF, N3831B
363	CL13	Mojave, Flight Systems, stored ex SAAF, N3842H
373	CL13	Mojave, Flight Systems, stored ex SAAF, N3844E
378	CL13	Mojave, Flight Systems, stored ex SAAF, N38453
380	CL13	Global Aerospace, ex SAAF, for sale N3846J
53-1328	F-86H	China Lake NAS
53-1396	F-86H	China Lake NAS
23238	CL13	Point Mugu NAS, on pylon preserved by ANG

Colorado

Serial	Type	Location
C123/52-4978	F-86F	Colorado Springs USAF Academy ex FA Argentina
51-2884	F-86F	Buckley ANG base - 120TFS area
53-782	F-86L	Peterson AFB, Space Command Museum
53-1308	F-86H	Lowry AFB, Heritage Museum

Connecticut

Serial	Type	Location
53-1367	F-86H	Meriden Possibly scrapped
53-1264	F-86H	Windsor Locks, New England Air Museum
120349	FJ1	Windsor Locks, New England Air Museum
48-263	F-86A	Windsor Locks, New England Air Museum

ex SAAF CL-13 now at Holloman with 6585TG (MAP)

ith F-86Fs from March 1957, when the first f some 90 were delivered. Attrition deliver-s followed, six Fiat-overhauled aircraft in ay/June 1960, and a further 19 by sea from e U.S. in January 1961. F-86Fs served with 31, 332, 334, 336 and 338 skvadrons until arch 1966, when the last skvadron received 5s.During latter years, the F-86Fs were stricted due to persistent wing cracking roblems, which have grounded other Sabres ound the world. Sixty U.S. built F-86Ks were urchased and delivered in September 1955, ough one machine was lost on acceptance ials in the U.S., and not replaced until nuary 1960. A hangar fire at Gardermoen n 10th March 1956 destroyed another four rcraft, and these were replaced by Fiat built abres three months later. RNoAF F-86K ini-ally equipped 337 and 339 skvadrons, but so replaced F-86Fs in 332 and 334 kvadrons at a later date. The last F-86Ks were ken off charge in 1968, and the majority rapped. The F-86Fs were largely ploughed ack into the MAP system, and went to such ountries as Saudi Arabia and Portugal. A fair w do remain in Norway, with some serving s 'swap' aircraft with the RNoAF Museum.

Pakistan: The Pakistan Air Force (PAF) saw lot of action with their Sabres over a 24 year an of service. The first of 120 F-86Fs was ccepted at Drigh Road in August 1956, and y 1958, all of this batch had been delivered. quadrons operating the F-86F included 5, 1, 14, 15, 16, 17, 18, 19, and 20 at the bases f Sargodha, Masroor and Faisal. In the 17 ay war with India in September 1965, these rcraft succeeded in shooting down Gnats, ampires, Hunters, Mysteres, and even a soli-ry Canberra. Many other Indian Aircraft ere destroyed on the ground by PAF Sabres. 1966, 90 ex-Luftwaffe Canadair Sabre 6s ere illegally obtained, via Iran. When the 971 war with India broke out, it was thought at the mix of US and Canadian -built Sabres ould be outclassed. However, again PAF abres saved the day, and succeeded in hooting down Indian Hunters, Sukhoi SU-7s nd Gnat/Adjeets. On December 11 1971, a AF Sabre shot down a supersonic MiG 21 ear Badin, a feat that was repeated on 17th ecember.Remaining Pakistani Sabres were ithdrawn in 1980, and many still linger on here, mainly as decoys.

Peru: The *Fuerza Aerea del Peru* (FAP) ceived 15 ex-USAF F-86Fs from July 1955, nd it is possible that others followed at a ter date. These Sabres were flown by scuadron de Caza 12 (later Grupo de Caza 2) at Limatambo. Wing spar cracks caused uite a few problems for the FAP, mainly due the F-86Fs flying mock combat missions ith Hunters, which also equipped Esc. de aza 12. In 1979-80, the Sabres were eplaced by the Sukhoi SU-22, and it is not nown if any Sabres remain here.

Philippines: The Philippine Air Force gained abre capability from 1957, when around 40 -86Fs began arriving, many from Taiwan.

Delaware		
53-1296	F-86H	Greater Wilmington Airport, Newcastle ANG base
District of Columbia		
53-134	F-86H	Washington, J.F. Kennedy playground
Florida		
53-728	F-86D	Dade County. Possibly scrapped.
52-5513	F-86F	Eglin AFB Armament Museum
143***	FJ4B	Chevalier Field, for Pensacola
120531	FJ1	Pensacola NAS Naval Aviation Museum
132023	FJ3	Pensacola NAS Naval Aviation Museum
139486	FJ4	Pensacola NAS Naval Aviation Museum
53-658	F-86L	Pinellas Park, Yesterdays Air Force
53-1255	F-86H	Fort Lauderdale in park
53-998	F-86L	Florida City, Highway 27
51-6059	F-86D	Indian Rocks Beach
53-4063	F-86L	Orange Park
143591	FJ4	Opa Locka Airport
52-10133	F-86D	Tyndall AFB, gate guard '45244'
Georgia		
51-5896	F-86D	Mercer Field, World Aircraft Museum
52-3651	F-86L	Georgia ANG base, Macon Municipal airport
53-1511	F-86H	Robins AFB Museum of Aviation
51-5891	F-86L	Georgia ANG base, Savannah International airport

47-615 at Rantoul AFB, Illinois (MAP)

Serving with 6, 7 and 9 Tactical Fighter Squadrons, F-86Ds arrived a year later, and 20 of these equipped an all-weather squadron. Though the D-model only saw ten years service, the F-86Fs served until about 1984, when three remaining examples were withdrawn at Basa. Many of the PAF Sabres went to a scrap yard near Basa, though other Sabres still live on in the Philippines.

Portugal: The _Força Aerea Portuguesa_ (FAP) took delivery of fifty F-86Fs in 1958. Another fifteen F-86Fs were purchased at a later date (Not Canadair Sabres, as has been reported). These Sabres were serialled 5301 to 5350 and 5351to 5365. The idea being that the first squadron, Esquadra 51, would operate the first 25 numerically, whilst Esquadra 52 would operate the next 25. Esc. 52 was short lived, however. Due to war in Africa, in 1961 Esc.52 Sabres were absorbed into Esc.51 and in August of that year, eight FAP Sabres deployed to Bissau Airport, Portuguese Guinea in a mission code named _Atlas_. The initial purpose was just to 'show the flag', but these aircraft eventually stayed until October 1964. Due to guerrilla activity at Port Guinea, FAP Sabres went into action as Close Air Support aircraft, and flew 577 missions. Though all bar one of the Sabres was hit by ground fire at one time or other, none were lost. Last operational mission in Portuguese Guinea was flown by Major Barbeitos de Sousa on 20th October 1964. When the Sabres left, their mission was taken over by the ubiquitous T-6! It had been foreseen that an FAP squadron would operated in Mozambique, flying ex-Luftwaffe Sabre 6s, but pressure from both the U.S. and Canadian Governments was brought to bear, and West Germany supplied Fiat G-91R 4s instead.Last FAP Sabres were withdrawn in July, 1980, when there were just six left in service at Monte Real. Aircraft were then swapped with various museums around Europe, and the _Museu do Ar_ at Alverca still keeps some F-86Fs for exchange.

Saudi Arabia: The Royal Saudi Air Force (RSAF) received sixteen F-86Fs in 1958, plus others at a later date, probably solely for spares use. These aircraft saw little usage, due to limited parts supply from the outset. Serving with 7 squadron, RSAF Sabres were phased out in the early 1970s. However, due to the attention that was focused on Saudi Arabia during the Gulf War, it has been discovered that a large number of these retired aircraft still survive at Dhahran, where as many as ten F-86Fs are to be found in a scrap area. A Sabre is also mounted on a pole here.

South Africa: The South African Air Force (SAAF) had the distinction of operating the Sabre twice, and under very different conditions. During the Korean War, the SAAF's No.2 _Cheetah_ squadron, attached to 18th FBW of the USAF, flew 22 F-86Fs from January 1953 until the end of the war. Six of these were written off, and the majority of the remainder was sent to the air force of Taiwan,

52-10057	F-86L	Valdosta town centre as 'MY'

Hawaii

50-653	F-86E	Hickam AFB
51-2841	F-86E	Hickam AFB ANG area
52-4191	F-86L	Hickam AFB, ANG area

Idaho

51-6074	F-86D	Blackfoot
53-1022	F-86D	Idaho Falls airport
52-10079	F-86D	Pocatello ex N59303

Illinois

51-6211	F-86D	Altamount
53-700	F-86L	Brookfield Park
51-6126	F-86D	Hillsboro
23338	CL13	Chanute AFB, RCAF colours ex 4689N
23351	CL13	Chanute AFB, RCAF colours ex N86ED
47-614	F-86A	Chanute AFB, Skyblazers colours
47-615	F-86A	Rantoul, on pylon

Indiana

52-2004	F-86H	Anderson park
52-5434	F-86F	Brazil County Legislature Building
53-1298	F-86H	Churnbusco park
50-632	F-86E	Indianapolis War Memorial
52-2058	F-86H	Grissom AFB heritage Museum MiG Alley Sally

Iowa

53-750	F-86L	Iowa City airport
52-3640	F-86D	Newton
53-924	F-86D	Urbandale

Kansas

	F-86	Wichita Airport Aviation Education center
52-4256	F-86L	McConnell AFB
53-718	F-86D	Hiawatha

Kentucky

52-3628	F-86D	Louisville Aircraft Industry museum
52-3694	F-86D	Sturgis

Louisiana

23226	CL13	England AFB, RCAF colours ex N46883
53-822	F-86D	Gretna
53-1029	F-86D	Ruston
53-1032	F-86D	White Castle
52-4168	F-86D	New Orleans ex Aero Nostalgia Stockton

Maryland

48-260	F-86A	Paul Garber Restoration facility NASM
53-1411	F-86H	Baltimore ANG base
53-1387	F-86H	Andrews AFB
53-1339	F-86H	Glenn L Martin field MD ANG
53-1348	F-86H	Clinton/Hyde Field. Possibly scrapped
52-2023	F-86H	Crisfield
52-2048	F-86H	Ellicott City
139536	FJ4	Bethesda
52-3864	F-86D	Lanham
52-2066	F-86H	Princess Anne

Massachusetts

53-1377	F-86H	Otis ANG museum

Michigan

52-5143	F-86F	Ypsilanti, Yankee Air Museum as '12852'
53-789	F-86D	Kellogg Airport Battle Creek
53-1096	F-86F	Kellogg Airport Battle Creek

through MAP.

In 1956, the SAAF renewed their association with the Sabre when they purchased 34 Canadair Sabre 6s for service with 1 and 2 squadrons. The last SAAF CL-13s flew with 85 Advanced Flying School at Pietersburg, which operated the type until April 1980. *Flight Systems* at Mojave, California then bought ten, but these aircraft were largely unused in FSI's drone programme, and at least one of these aircraft is now for sale. An ex-SAAF Sabre 6 was also operated in Europe as part of a NATO target - towing contract from 1988, until it's return to the USA with *Corporate Jet* in late 1992.

Spain: The Ejercito del Aire(EdA) was a major operator of the F-86F, and operated 244 of the type. The EdA equipped around 14 Escuadrons with the F-86F, but many of these squadron numbers were the result of renumbering existing Escuadrons. F-104Gs took over from 1965, with F-5s following later, and the last EdA Sabres were withdrawn on the last day of 1972. There are numerous Sabres left here, including examples at the excellent *Museo del Aire* near Madrid, and thirty or so in various states of explosive disrepair on the Las Bardenas ranges.

Taiwan: A look through the list of Chinese Nationalist Air Force (CNAF) F-86Fs is like a look through the 'Who's Who?' of the Korean War. Jim Thompson's *The Huff*, Joseph McConnells *Beautious Butch*, Harold Fischer's *Paper Tiger* and Ralp Parr's *Barb/Vente de la Morte* were all among the 320 F-86Fs which went to Taiwan in 1955. These combat veterans saw action again in 1958, when they fought mainland-Chinese based MiG 17s over the Straits of Formosa. 29 enemy jets were downed for no reported losses. As late as 1977, there were still 100 or more F-86Fs flying in Taiwan, though a small number of F-86Ds had been replaced by F-100s. It is thought that two reserve squadrons flew the Sabre until well into the 1980's and many may well survive in this corner of the world. Only one F-86F is definitely known to be preserved, however.

Thailand: The Royal Thai Air Force (RTAF) received 40 F-86Fs from 1961, serving with 13 and 43 squadrons. They were replaced by F-5s in 1966. Thailand was the only export customer for the F-86L (updated F-86D), which featured a ground to air datalink and extended span wings, similar to the F-86F-40 series. Operating with 12 squadron from 1964, 20 of these aircraft flew with RTAF until also being replaced by F-5s.Around ten Sabres of both models are known to exist in Thailand, though it is possible that more decoy airframes are in use.

Tunisia: 15 F-86Fs were obtained by Tunisia in 1969, presumably for use as fighter bombers. Despite rumours that a dozen or so arrived from Arizona in 1983, it is thought that Tunisian Sabres were totally replaced by the Aermacchi MB 326K in 1978. No survivors are known.

53-4028	F-86D	Birmingham
53-663	F-86D	Mount Clemens
49-1095	F-86A	Selfridge ANG base, military air museum
50-480	F-86E	Detroit Willow Run airport
Minnesota		
52-5757	F-86	Fairmount, Route 16
51-6038	F-86	Luverne park
Mississippi		
51-5908	F-86D	Gulfport
53-1061	F-86D	Jackson, Interstate 55
Missouri		
52-4181	F-86D	Kansas City
52-1983	F-86D	La Plata
53-946	F-86D	Poplar Bluff
52-3887	F-86D	Washington
53-1250	F-86H	Spirit Fighters, Chesterfield. Rebuild to fly
Montana		
47-637	F-86A	Great Falls ANG base on pylon
Nebraska		
52-3735	F-86L	Lincoln ANG base wreck
53-831	F-86L	Lincoln ANG base, Municipal airport
53-1503	F-86H	McCook
53-1375	F-86H	Offutt AFB, SAC Museum
Nevada		
53-994	F-86D	Reno, Stead airport
53-1045	F-86L	Battle Mountain Museum
New Mexico		
51-13010	F-86E	Cannon AFB memorial park
53-1251	F-86H	Cannon AFB Memorial park
50-459	F-86D	Clayton/Fort Jordan Museum
51-13028	F-86E	Holloman AFB
52-3646	F-86D	Roswell Museum
67 x F-86H and L models		NM Institute of Mining and Technology, Socorro
New York		
135868	FJ3	New York Intrepid air sea and space museum
48-200	F-86A	Clay
51-2986	F-86D	Islip
52-10052	F-86D	Monroe/Waterloo
53-1272	F-86H	harlem, 118th Street and 5th Avenue
143610	FJ4B	Buffalo
52-3702	F-86L	Stewart AFB
53-1337	F-86L	Shortsville Legion Hall
53-1306	F-86H	Suffolk County AFB
53-1519	F-86H	Syracuse ANG base
53-134*	F-86H	White Plains
North Carolina		
50-600	F-86E	Charlotte International airport
52-4142	F-86D	Charlotte ANG base on pylon
53-919	F-86D	Maxton
53-1007	F-86D	Wilmington AFB
53-1370	F-86H	Seymour Johnson AFB as '112972'
141393	FJ3M	Hickory Municipal airport, Sabre Society
North Dakota		
53-719	F-86D	Grand Forks
53-1253	F-86H	Jamestown

Turkey: The Turkish Aur Force/*Turk Hava Kuvvetleri* (THK) operated a variety of Sabres from July 1954, when the first of 102 CL-13 Mk.2s arrived. These aircraft were possibly bolstered by a small number of F-86Fs later, and served 141, 142, and 143 squadrons at Merzifon and Eskisehir. A number (possibly as many as 50) of F-86Ds were obtained in the early 1960's, and both variants flew until 1968-69. Only a handful of Sabre 2s are known to exist at present, and no F-86Ds are thought to have survived, but further information would be very helpful.

United Kingdom: The Royal Air Force (RAF) went swept winged from May 1953, when 427 Canadair Sabre 4s plus three Mk. 2s were ferried across the Atlantic. The RAF equipped 3, 4, 20, 26, 67, 71, 93, 112, 130 and 234 squadrons in West Germany as well as 66 and 92 squadrons in the UK. However, Sabres were only a stop-gap fighter until Hawker Hunters became available, and the first of these arrived in August 1955, and in just a year, all squadrons had re-equipped. Some aircraft were scrapped, but a large number went to Italy and Yugoslavia. One that did remain was XB982, which was converted into an Orpheus engine test bed by Bristol Siddeley. In this guise it flew between November 1959 and some time in 1960. This was the last Sabre to operated in the UK until F-86A G-SABR was imported early in 1992. Another ex-RAF Sabre was imported from Italy in 1967 by the *Historic Aircraft Preservation Society*. XB733 was registered as G-ATBF and after many moves, ended up on a farm near Preston, Lancashire.

United States of America: The USAF Sabre story really is too complicated to easily recount here. Basically, the USAF flew the F-86A from March 1949, the F-86E from February 1951, the F-86F from March 1952, the F-86H from November 1954, the F-86D from March 1952, and the F-86L from October 1956. The Sabre equipped 150 front line squadrons plus 57 Air National Guard (ANG) squadrons. The U.S.A. was also the sole operator of the FJ-Fury series, which developed from a need for a Navalised Sabre. The last flight by a Sabre of an active U.S. military squadron was by an F-86H of the Maryland ANG on 4th August 1970. Many ex - ANG F-86Hs went to Navy squadron VX-4 at Point Mugu or to China Lake for the drone programme. Retired Sabres went on display outside Legion Halls, Schools and Government buildings, and this has assured a good supply of restorable airframes. Unfortunately, these aircraft had their main spars cut to prevent them flying again, and for this reason, the majority of flying Sabres in the U.S. today have come from overseas.

Venezuela: The Fuerza Aerea Venezolana (FAV) took delivery of 30 F-86F-30s from October 1955 to December 1960, in three batches. One squadron was equipped: Escuadron de Caza 36. On 1st January 1958, these aircraft flew low over Caracas and

Ohio

53-1023	F-86D	Bradner/Rising Sun
53-1528	F-86H	Lunkin airport
52-3831	F-86D	Dayton, Carrillon park
49-1067	F-86A	Dayton/Wright Patterson AFB USAFM
50-477	F-86D	Dayton USAFM 97FIS as Dennis the Menace
53-1352	F-86H	Dayton USAFM, sectioned
53-1058	F-86D	Franklin
53-959	F-86L	Newbury, Soplata Collection
53-715	F-86L	Newbury, Soplata Collection
	F-86E	Newbury, Soplata Collection
52-3719	F-86D	Struthers
51-3048	F-86D	Tiffin
52-2059	F-86H	Toledo/Sylvania
52-3814	F-86D	Uhrichsville
53-724	F-86D	Urbana airport
53-944	F-86D	Van Wert

Oklahoma

53-773	F-86D	Kingfisher
52-10142	F-86D	McAlester
	F-86K?	Stroud (reported as 53-8277 which w/o Italy
51-8409	F-86D	Brown Field, Tulsa ANG base gate guard

Oregon

51-6055	F-86D	Hill AFB, ex Albany
51-3024	F-86D	Astoria
51-8467	F-86D	Corvallis
	F-86D	Troutdale, Bob Sturges, Cherry Pk rd
53-781	F-86D	Vale
52-4755	F-86F	Clackamas, Oregon Military museum ex ROKAF

Pennsylvania

52-2065	F-86H	Avon
53-1338	F-86H	Erie airport, Interstate 90
52-2043	F-86H	Freeport
53-665	F-86D	Imperial route 22
53-1316	F-86H	Philipsburgh
53-894	F-86L	Greater Pittsburgh IAP ANG Collection
52-10046	F-86D	Sadsburyville
143568	FJ4B	Willow Grove NAS museum
51-13417	F-86F	Reading, Mid Atlantic Air Museum ex C5-235 Spanish

South Carolina

141376	FJ3	Beaufort MCAS
53-1386	F-86H	McEntire AFB, 169TFG Museum
53-1064	F-86L	McEntire AFB, 169TFG Museum
52-1976	F-86H	Greenville
52-5737	F-86H	Florence Air & Space Museum
132057	FJ2	Patriots Point, USS Yorktown Museum

South Dakota

53-1302	F-86H	Ellsworth AFB
	F-86D	Sturgis as '29632'

Tennessee

52-3679	F-86D	Knoxville
52-3840	F-86D	Lookout Mountain
53-635	F-86D	Memphis Airport
53-668	F-86D	Nashville Bicentennial park

Texas

52-4492	F-86F	Bergstrom AFB, gate guard
52-3770	F-86D	Austin ANG HQ
53-3693	F-86D	Breckenridge
53-1030	F-86D	Dallas, Addison airport NAS Collection
51-2826	F-86E	Flying Tiger Air Museum, Paris
	F-86D	Flying Tiger Air Museum, Paris
52-3749	F-86D	Del Rio Airport